GUNZ AND GOD

The Life of an NYPD Undercover

By Stevie Stryker
and
Rocco Parascandola

ISBN: 978-1-4834-4589-2 (sc)
ISBN: 978-1-4834-4590-8 (e)

Lulu Publishing Services rev. date: 05/19/2016

CONTENTS

DEDICATION

This book is dedicated to undercover police officers everywhere. They toil in necessary anonymity and garner little public acknowledgment for a job as important as it is dangerous.

Detective Stevie Stryker. Credit: *New York Daily News.*

PROLOGUE

Undercover NYPD Detective Stevie Stryker* got behind the wheel of the black Lexus, ready as ever to go buy some guns.

Next to him was Detective Leroy Dressler.* He was relatively new to undercover work, had never before partnered with Stryker and had never worked a gun case.

"We're getting something bigger," Stryker told Dressler. "We're getting something more than you normally get. I pray before I go out because I believe in a higher power protecting us, and I pray I don't get hurt and I don't have to kill anyone."

A deeply religious man, Stryker tried not to wear it on his sleeve. God talk, he knew, made many people, cops no exception, a little uncomfortable.

But Dressler surprised him.

"I pray, too," he told Stryker.

**Author's note: Stevie Stryker is a pseudonym, indicated by an asterisk (*) and meant to protect his identity. The names of other police officers deeply involved in narcotics operations, as well as the names of Stryker's family members, have also been changed.*

Both men bowed their heads down.

"Lord protect us from our enemies and let us not hurt our enemies," Stryker said, "nor allow our enemies to hurt us."

Game time.

Stryker turned on the radio, Hot 97 FM. Rap music, as if any more adrenaline was needed.

"We drop the windows down, blast the music and we are on our way," Stryker said. "We get to the Bronx. The informant is there. The informant doesn't know we're actually undercovers. He thinks we're bad guys and the informant is setting us up for a legit deal, not realizing we're cops."

At the housing project where the sale was set to take place, the detectives quickly learned from the informant, a guy in his 20s named Danny, that there were nine guns for sale, not two, as originally discussed. That would make for a stronger case in court. It also meant more chance of bloodshed.

"I remember telling Detective Dressler, 'Don't talk while we're in there,'" Stryker said. "I was like, 'I'll do the talking. Do not sit with me. Stand off to the side just in case something goes bad because I'll deal with whatever's in front of me. You deal with whatever's in front of you, but we will not sit together.'

"I also told him they might try to get us in separate rooms so they can go at us in separate conversations to see if our story's right. So we have to be two steps ahead of them."

The detectives got on the elevator with Danny. Before the doors closed another guy slipped inside. Stryker didn't know him. Danny did.

"Money Mike, what's up?"

Guys with names like Money Mike generally aren't 9-to-5 office workers. They usually don't play by the rules. They have criminal records. And they are not nice guys.

He clearly was there for the gun buy.

Stryker was nervous. Who invited him to the party? Why was he on the elevator? Were we being set up?

The detectives would later learn that the mini-transmitter in Stryker's cell phone – the wire, or kel, as it is formally known – had gone dead, cutting off communication with their back-up team, also known as the field team.

No surprise there.

For all the gizmos and gadgets now used by most big police departments in America, including the NYPD, technology at the start of the 21st century was still a major concern in New York City. Radios often failed in the subway. And kels often didn't work in bad weather, in the subway and in buildings with thick concrete walls. Such as the one Stryker and Dressler were standing in.

"Thank God the elevator's working," Stryker told Danny, unaware his back-up team couldn't hear him. "How far would we have to walk if it wasn't?"

"We're going to 12," Danny said.

Cool, Stryker thought to himself, unaware that his back-up didn't know the deal was on the 12th floor.

The ride went smoothly. They stepped off on 12 and Money Mike banged on an apartment door.

A woman answered.

Not typical, but it was her apartment.

Whatever. It was on.

"There are about four people sitting in the living room," Stryker said. "There are pounds of coke on the table with bags and scales. It is definitely a drug den. Danny said, 'I'm gonna go get the guy with the guns.' I'm slapping everybody five. 'Yo, what up? I'm Stevie.'"

An older man, maybe 60, was sitting on a chair and cutting up coke laid out on a table in front of him. Oddly, there was a boy, the woman's son, nine years old at the most, watching TV and oblivious to all around him.

Dressler took his post by the door.

"Have a seat," someone said.

Dressler played like a wooden Indian. Didn't say boo. Didn't move.

"He's good," Stryker said. "His job is to watch me. His doesn't need to be sitting with me. He's got hemorrhoids."

Laughs all around.

Meanwhile, there was a shotgun on the table that was clearly meant to intimidate the detectives.

Stryker wasn't fazed.

"That didn't make me nervous," Stryker said. "I always tell guys – get nervous when you can't see the drugs and the guns."

Dressler, however, was beyond scared.

He was honored that Stryker had enlisted him in the operation. On Dressler's first day in narcotics Stryker was one of several undercovers to offer advice and help whenever it was needed. Dressler took him up on the offer. He never thought Stryker would be coming to *him* for help, but just an hour earlier Stryker found out his steady partner couldn't work that day. Stryker could have postponed the buy. Danny would have understood. He and Stryker had done business before and Danny had come to believe Stryker was exactly who he said he was, a bad guy looking to buy guns. But Stryker decided against that. In fact, he was all set to make the buy himself. And he likely would have done just that were it not for Sergeant Rob Skellman.*

Every undercover needs a good handler, a supervisor who can coax the best work out of the undercover, push him to do better, ease up on the criticism when necessary and generally make the tough decisions to ensure everyone gets home alive.

Skellman was that guy for Stryker. He'd been around the block. He'd been involved in shootings. And he'd spent a large chunk of his career supervising undercovers. He knew full well the dangers of overconfidence, of arrogance. He wanted none of this. Sure, Stryker had developed a rapport with Danny. But Danny was no different than any other dealer – he got used to a pattern, to a certain way of doing things.

He was, in fact, just like most of us, a creature of habit. If Stryker showed up alone, the shit could have easily hit the fan if Danny's mind started racing. Was Stryker solo because his sidekick got arrested? Did he flip on Stryker? Was Stryker now cooperating? Was he wearing a wire?

And if so, might Danny just figure, in the heat of the moment, that he'd play the odds, pull his piece and put two in Stryker's skull?

All of that took Skellman two seconds to analyze. Go get yourself another undercover, he told Stryker.

Assigned to the Major Case Unit of Manhattan North Narcotics, Stryker was based in a four-story Harlem building that also housed other NYPD units. On any given day, several hundred cops of all stripes, ranks and talents were there.

"I'm walking through the building, just searching for anybody that was an undercover that could go with me," Stryker said. "Is that a good thing? No, because you're bringing someone new into a major deal not really knowing how they're going to handle the pressure of what you're doing.

"The guys on the lower floor were into the dime bags and weed bags and $2 bags of crack, but I'm gonna grab somebody to buy two guns, and I was also supposed to buy over 100 grams of coke. But it's the guns that change the pressure. So I gotta find someone who can step up to that."

Dressler at that point in his career was doing drug buy and busts in the 28th Precinct, in another part of Harlem. Important work, to be sure, but nothing like buying guns. Still, he looked the part – 5 feet 10 inches tall, solidly built – a black belt, in fact. Muscle for a skinny guy like Stryker.

"But I wasn't really sure what I'm supposed to do," Dressler said. "So I just stand by the door and watch Stevie. I'm impressed. He's confident. He's talking with these guys like he's known them for years. I just don't know what he wants me to do."

A knock on the door.

Another guy entered.

He had the two original guns – a 9mm handgun and a TEC-9 submachine gun – plus seven others up for grabs. Stryker wanted them all.

"One guy with a shotgun wants $400. I say, 'I'll give you $200,'" Stryker told them. "Then the guy with the two guns said, 'I got other guns.' Danny comes in with another guy. He's got a couple of guns. I'm checking them all out."

Dressler couldn't believe his eyes.

"What's impressive is Steve's ability to be able to control what was going on in the room. He sees the guns and it's, 'Oh, let me see that gun.' Now, he's got the gun in his hands. 'You got bullets? You got bullets?'"

If Dressler was unsure of himself, Stryker felt otherwise, even when the sellers suggested a trip to the roof to test the guns.

"Of course, as a cop I can't do that," Stryker said. "Plus, it puts me farther away from my back-up. I might get thrown off the roof. I don't know who else is up there. And, check this out: What if cops are doing a vertical? Then what? I'm gonna get shot by friendly fire?"

Vertical patrols are a staple of how cops fight crime in apartment buildings, especially the city-run housing projects.

Verticals, as they are best known, involve two cops taking an elevator to the top floor of a building, then slowly walking down the stairs, stopping at each floor to look for trespassers, drug dealers, loiterers and other troublemakers.

It is a remarkably unsophisticated, yet highly effective, police tactic.

And dangerous as hell.

In February 2016, two Bronx cops were shot and wounded by a man they stopped to question in a housing project stairwell. More than a year before that, in November 2014, a rookie Brooklyn cop, stepping into a darkened stairwell in a housing project in East New York, one of the city's toughest neighborhoods, was startled by a noise one floor below and unintentionally pulled the trigger on his already-drawn 9mm Glock. The bullet struck the wall, then ricocheted and struck and killed a young unarmed man who had just entered the stairwell with his girlfriend.

But at that moment, whatever fear Stryker had he tried his best to keep to himself.

"What I tell them is how stupid it would be to go to the roof, shoot the guns then get caught," he said.

By now, the group was comfortable with Stryker. They agreed – it would make no sense to go to the roof. Fuck that.

Let's eat instead, they told him. Have a drink. Relax. We'll do our business in a little while.

Stryker would have loved to, but he knew the moment he let his guard down someone could be lacing his meal with God knows what.

He declined. Then his phone rang.

It was Skellman.

He was unflappable, regardless of circumstance. But his job was to worry, to prepare for every possible contingency, to fret about things no one else considered. If he brought everyone home safe then thank God for that. And if guns, drugs and arrests came with that, well, that was all the better.

But Skellman wasn't calling to see what Stryker wanted for lunch. Stryker knew the only reason for Skellman to call him in the middle of a buy was because there was a problem with the wire.

Skellman, not sure what danger Stryker might be facing – or if one of the dealers had grabbed the phone to answer it – was careful not to tip his hand.

"Yo, Stevie, what's happening?" Skellman asked.

Stryker froze.

###########

The NYPD is the biggest police force in America, a vast and sprawling agency of more than 35,000 officers, plus another 15,000 civilian employees. It has 77 precincts, 12 transit districts, nine Housing Bureau commands, plus scores of other units – Anti-Crime, the Central Robbery Task Force, Vice Enforcement, Harbor, Scuba, and on and on and on.

Then there are the less dangerous assignments, in theory at least. You like animals? Ride a horse as a member of the Mounted Unit. You a former pilot? Join the Aviation Unit? The department even has two beekeepers, one a detective who typically works on counterterrorism cases and the other a patrol officer.

And let's not forget the myriad paper-pushing positions. Every precinct has an administrative lieutenant, an integrity control officer and a desk sergeant. If you work inside they call you a "house mouse." But you work steady hours and you clock in fairly confident you won't be staring at a gun in your face that day.

Stryker could have been one of those guys. Sign in. Wear a uniform. Keep a stack of take-out menus in the desk drawer. As a kid, he dreamed of becoming a lawyer. The vague, nebulous dream of a teenager – he knew they made a lot of money. And after leaving the military he worked in a bank, for God's sake. But if he did the suit-and-tie thing it'd be like sitting on the sidelines. The players want to play. Make a difference. Change the world.

"I hate guns," he said. "I mean, I truly hate them. When I take a gun off the street, somebody's not getting shot with that gun. Some grandmother's not getting hit by a stray bullet. Some kid's not getting shot on the way home from school. That's how I look at it."

############

The wire was dead. Not good but not uncommon. Like a running back reversing course when his blocking breaks down, Stryker didn't miss a beat.

"Yo, Uncle Skell, what's up?...Yeah, I'm good. I'm gonna need more money later on. I'm getting some good product up here."

Then he hung up.

Or so he made it seem, leaving his phone on for the rest of the deal.

All good, Skellman, on the other end of the line, thought to himself. He and Stryker had in advance agreed that if a problem arose, if Stryker needed help and back-up needed to be sent in, he'd complain about what was happening inside the apartment.

"If he said, 'My Uncle Skell isn't going to like this,' I'd know there was a problem," Skellman said.

Fortunately, the dealers weren't looking to rob Stryker and Dressler. With Skellman listening in the whole time the detectives finished up business and walked out of there without a scratch, their guns stashed in laundry bags, 100 grams of coke in Stryker's pocket.

"Stevie Gunz!" a colleague yelled out when he and Dressler returned to the office and unpacked their haul.

A nickname was born.

"If he was trying to impress me that day that's just what he did," Dressler said. "That was just him. He could sell heat to the devil and ice to the ice man."

The investigation, meanwhile, would continue for a few more months, and in the end a dozen suspects would be arrested, including the woman in whose apartment the deal went down.

In a perverse way, Stryker said, she was a halfway decent mother, never leaving her kid alone if she couldn't find a sitter.

"The child was with us a couple of times when we later went to buy drugs a couple of blocks away. She was like the steerer for that crew. She would take me to go get drugs, coke. When we got there she would point me to someone else she was working with. The boy would sit in the car."

Stryker, a father himself, felt for the kid.

"One day, I wind up asking this little boy where his dad was."

"Minnesota."

"You ever talk to your dad?"

"Sometimes."

"I bet you don't remember your dad's number."

"Yes," the boy insisted. "I do."

He said the number out loud. Stryker typed it into his phone and locked it in.

"The day of the takedown I called his ass personally to tell him what happened and told him, 'You're coming to New York to get your son.'"

Looking back on the day of the big buy, however, Stryker wasn't so brash.

"Scary," he said. "We were lucky to get out of there alive."

CHAPTER 1 – DOUBLE EXECUTION

The gun buy was about to go horribly wrong.

"What's the big deal?" Detective James Nemorin asked Ronell Wilson. "Everybody's leery. Listen, I'm leery. I'm leery, too. I understand. I don't want to get caught up."

If Nemorin was scared, it didn't necessarily show in his voice. He was a pro, he and the guy next to him, the one pretending to be his brother-in-law, Detective Rodney Andrews.

They were go-to guys in the NYPD's Firearms Investigations Unit. A year earlier, in 2002, the vaunted unit took 484 guns off the streets, up from 186 in 2000. Even with its recent expansion, the FIU, as it was best known, was still cream-of-the crop.

This particular case on Staten Island, run-of-the-mill in so many ways up to that point, seemed headed to its most typical conclusion: Hands on your head, asshole. You're under arrest.

Just a few days earlier, in fact, Nemorin had bought a .357 Magnum from a dealer named Omar Green. A trust level had been established.

Or so it appeared.

Green then agreed to sell Nemorin a TEC-9 submachine gun. But in the middle of a cold night in March, Nemorin had some explaining to do. Not to Green but rather to two accomplices, Ronell Wilson, 20, and his muscle, Jesse Jacobus, 17 years old and 300 pounds. Both were members of the Stapleton Crew, a street gang.

They were sitting in Nemorin's Nissan Maxima. At least one of them was armed, the cops likely figured. And Wilson was not happy. Who, he wanted to know of Nemorin, was the guy sitting next to you?

"There's nothing to worry about," Detective Nemorin said with the lilt of his Haitian homeland. "Look, we're not going to deal in front of him, OK? I'm coming. I could step out and we do the deal outside."

In truth, there was plenty to worry about. Wilson and Jacobus were in the back seat, a cardinal sin in the world of undercover work. Never, ever let the bad guys get behind you. Of course, what's taught in a controlled setting doesn't always translate to the streets. Real police work is never quite how they draw it up in the classroom. How that happened with Nemorin or Andrews, whether it was a tactical error or something out of their control, will likely never be fully known.

Wilson and Jacobus, it was later revealed, had no intention of selling Nemorin the TEC-9. There may have been suspicion among the gang members that Nemorin was NYPD. At the very least, they planned to rob the detective of the $1,200 he was carrying for the gun deal.

The verbal sparring played out during an uneasy car ride in which the detectives sent a signal to the field team that one of the four surveillance cars following them had been spotted and needed to back off.

The tension in the car was palpable.

It got worse when Wilson ordered the detectives to pull over in front of Green's house, ostensibly so Wilson could pick up the TEC-9. Wilson and Jacobus got out of the car. That forced the cops in the surveillance cars to drive past to avoid being detected. Moments later, the back-up team heard Wilson and Jacobus over the wire telling Nemorin and Andrews they were going to search them.

The partners played dumb.

Search us? Why? For what reason?

"I'm the nigger in charge," Wilson snapped back, pulling out a .44-caliber handgun.

The next moments would shock the city.

############

To live in New York City after September 11th, 2001, was to live in a different world. Life-changing in ways large and small.

The NYPD, of course, was a large part of that change. The terror attack had occurred on the day of the mayoral Democratic primary, and after it was pushed back two weeks, Mayor Rudolph Giuliani sought a 90-day extension that would allow him to stay in office past the end of the year.

A man never known for his restraint, Giuliani also threatened to challenge the city's term limits law and run for another four-year term if the primary candidates didn't permit the extension. Who better to lead us than the man dubbed "America's Mayor" for his steadfast demeanor as New York City tried to recover from the attack? At least, that's what his supporters said. A transition to a new mayor, the reasoning went, regardless who got the job, would disrupt the city even further. Even the two leading candidates for mayor – Republican Michael Bloomberg and Democrat Mark Green – thought it was a good idea.

Giuliani's detractors – and there were many – called it a naked power grab by a man trying to remake his scarred legacy. Indeed, Giuliani on September 10th was a man in decline, weakened by prostate cancer, estranged from his wife and hated by a good percentage of New Yorkers, most notably minorities.

In truth, New York State's constitution allowed for emergency extensions. But in the end, with polls showing public support for term limits, State Assembly Speaker Sheldon Silver threw cold water on Giuliani's plan, noting a great majority of the 99 Democrats in the 150-member Assembly opposed the extension.

Life went on, as normal as it possibly could under the circumstances, and Bloomberg was elected mayor. His choice for police commissioner was a blast from the past, Raymond Kelly, who had served as the city's top cop under Mayor David Dinkins and helped run the probe that led to the conviction of those who bombed the World Trade Center in 1993.

But Kelly later got bounced from his perch at One Police Plaza as Giuliani defeated Dinkins when he ran for a second term and chose Bill Bratton to lead the nation's largest police force.

When Kelly returned for his second stint as commissioner he had even more experience under his belt. Under President Bill Clinton he was the U.S. Treasury Department's undersecretary for enforcement, then later the head of the U.S. Customs Service. He knew from that experience, however, that the cooperation between federal and local authorities was not always what it should be. New York City, he believed, would not and could not rely primarily on Washington, D.C., to protect it.

Thus came an expansion of the NYPD's Intelligence Division, a sharp increase in the number of investigators assigned to the Joint Terrorism Task Force, which is run by the FBI and is comprised of representatives from numerous law enforcement agencies, and the creation of the Counterterrorism Bureau, a first for a municipal police agency.

More than a decade later, how police in New York City conduct surveillance of Muslims remains a hot topic. Detractors believe the NYPD engages in profiling and illegal surveillance. The NYPD and its supporters say police act within the framework of the law and the constitution, gleaning information from open-source material available on the Internet and attending meetings and events that any New Yorker could.

And there has not been a single successful large-scale terrorist attack in the city since 2001, they note. As Kelly was remaking the NYPD, conventional crime, remarkably, continued to fall. And even as New Yorkers fretted about another terror attack, they were lulled into a sense that the street crime that ravaged the city in the 1970s, 80s and early 90s – through the fiscal crisis, the availability of guns and the crack era – was a thing of the past.

###########

Without warning, Jacobus would later testify, Wilson shot Andrews, point blank in the head, and then turned his attention to Nemorin.

"Where's the shit?" Wilson wanted to know. "Where's the money?"

"He was pleading for his life," Jacobus said of Nemorin.

Then Wilson executed him.

"Blood was everywhere," Jacobus said. "On the seats. On the windows."

Andrews, shield number 1034, married, two sons, known to colleagues as Jay. Dead. Nemorin, shield number 6690, married, three kids, known to colleagues as the "Haitian Sensation," for his flashy wardrobe. Dead.

Wilson and Jacobus got out of the car and walked away.

Then they stopped, walked back, pulled the two detectives from the car, took Nemorin's gun and drove off. The bodies of the two slain officers, the first killed in the line of duty since the day the Twin Towers fell, were found minutes later when their back-up discovered them, lying at Hannah Street and St. Paul's Avenue. And just like that, a seemingly routine operation in a corner of the city that most New Yorkers knew little about had turned into a tragedy. Any notion that the only criminals to be worried about had Middle Eastern names and wanted to commit acts of terror was quickly dispelled.

Sergeant Richard Abbate, who supervised Nemorin and Andrews, later revealed in court his worst moments as a police officer.

"I saw that [Andrews] had one eye closed and one eye opened," he said at Wilson's trial. "He had sustained a wound to his head. I then approached Detective Nemorin. There was a long line of blood coming from his head."

All told, eight men, including Wilson, Jacobus and Green, were charged in the sensational case. Seven pleaded guilty. While in prison,

Wilson fathered a son, "Justus," with a prison guard, Nancy Gonzalez. Police and federal prosecutors said it was part of a ploy to gain sympathy and avoid the death sentence.

It didn't work. Wilson was convicted and sentenced to death, the first such sentence by a federal jury in New York City since bank robber Gerhard Puff was electrocuted in 1954 for killing a FBI agent. Wilson offered no words of remorse for his victims' families, instead sticking out his tongue in an act of defiance.

But he was eventually spared death when a federal judge ruled that the convicted killer was too intellectually disabled to be executed.

When Stryker heard the news about Nemorin and Andrews he felt a pit in his stomach, the way any cop does when a fellow officer is killed.

"I knew them as undercover brothers," Stryker said. "We all belong to a fraternity of undercovers."

But there was more to Stryker's grief than that. A day before Nemorin and Andrews were killed, Stryker and Dressler met up with Calvin Turner, a 54-year-old violent ex-con who had done time for manslaughter. He had shot a 19-year-old woman during a residential burglary, then later killed a fellow inmate in prison with an ice pick. Back out on the street, he was going to sell Stryker and Dressler three guns for $1,200.

The detectives knew from their training: always control the situation, never let the dealer tell you who you can and can't bring to a buy and never ever let the bad guy get behind you. Not on the street, and certainly not in a vehicle. But Turner, whose past also included selling drugs to an undercover, was no stranger to this dance.

"We pull up and we allowed him to jump in the back seat and ride with us," Stryker remembered. "It was a plain, stupid mistake. We were overconfident and it could have cost us. He could have shot us both and left. Why not? He thought we were thugs.

"But God spared us."

############

Stryker at that point had been an undercover since 1996. His star was rising steadily. In 2002, with more than 500 narcotics buys and more than 25 gun buys under his belt, he was promoted from detective third-grade to detective second-grade.

"Detective Stryker sets the bar for all incoming undercovers into the Organized Crime Control Bureau as he leads by example using his wealth of narcotics knowledge and experience, which he has compiled in six years of undercover work," a NYPD captain wrote is support of Stryker's promotion. "Detective Stryker is an asset….to the entire New York City Police Department."

Kelly called him a top-notch investigator. Joseph Esposito, who served as Chief of Department under Kelly, remembered a cop who lived for the chase and loved taking guns off the streets. And Jordan Arnold, who as a Manhattan assistant district attorney successfully prosecuted a number of cases in which Stryker was the lead undercover, said Stryker could take on whatever persona was necessary.

"A lot of guys can't do that," Arnold said. "They can play a mob guy, let's say, but nothing else. Stevie could adapt to any situation."

Another prosecutor, Anthony Capozzolo, agreed with that assessment. He also said Stryker's boyish looks – when he was 35 he looked like a teenager – and slight frame were a tremendous asset.

"His looks definitely worked for him," Capozzolo said. "No one thought he was going to rob them. In fact, there'd always be the worry dealers would try to rob *him*, but that wouldn't make sense for them. Why rob the golden goose? He's bringing them all this business."

For Stryker, it didn't matter if he was needed for a case he wasn't involved in, even if it was in another borough of the city. He was a sought-after asset and would often be called in to help out with cases not being handled by the unit to which he was assigned.

Heady stuff, for sure, and enough to go to your head. Stryker, he admitted, would sometimes let the compliments of others do just that, even though as an undercover his work was invisible to the general public and known only to those with whom he worked.

"You get cocky," he said. "You think you're Superman. Nothing can happen to me. It's hard, because you gotta be confident. You're selling yourself – they gotta believe you're one of them. Dealing guns. Buying guns. So, sometimes you slip up and go too far. You get sloppy."

His success as an undercover had bred overconfidence, if not arrogance. No assignment, he felt, was impossible. Oddly, his faith in God had played a role in his attitude, though Stryker knew deep down that no God of any faith approves of hubris. Be humble, Stryker had been taught since he was a child. It wasn't always so easy for him to remember that.

"I always felt everything would be OK because I had God on my side," Stryker said. "But there were times when I let my success go to my head. No doubt.

"One time I had coke in my front pocket, dope from another drug deal in another pocket, a gun in another pocket from a third deal. Another time, I wanted to go out on a buy when I didn't even have someone to back me up. The sarge said there was no way he was letting me go out there. And I said, 'So what? I'm Stevie Gunz.'"

So in character was Gunz that he'd too often get home and greet his wife Charlene and kids like the criminal he was paid to imitate.

"Yo, sup?"

Imagine Robert De Niro as Travis Bickle in "Taxi Driver?"

"You talking to me, honey? You talking to me?"

The wife, of course, would have none of that.

"Go back outside," she would say, "check that attitude at the door and come back in like a normal person."

"Yes, dear."

"Hi, sweetie. How was your day? Is that better?"

"Yes. Now throw out the garbage."

############

And so the murders of Nemorin and Andrews provided a hard dose of reality Stryker did not soon forget. Nearly seven years into his career as an undercover, he had learned a lesson in humility. For someone who had a growing sense of invincibility, it was a lesson worth remembering.

CHAPTER 2 – BORN IN BROOKLYN

In September 2012, former President Bill Clinton, his wife Hillary and their daughter Chelsea dined at Roberta's, a trendy, highly-acclaimed pizzeria restaurant in the Bushwick section of Brooklyn. The idea would have seemed laughable 20 years earlier and utterly ridiculous 20 years before that, when Stryker was growing up during a time of high crime and social upheaval.

Bushwick was founded by Peter Stuyvesant in 1661, one of the original six towns settled by the Dutch. Bushwick comes from the word "boswijck," which means thick woods. Out of the woods, farms were created, later replaced by various manufacturing firms – sugar, oil and glue, among them.

By the late 1840s, the German immigrants who flooded the area brought with them their passion for beer. In its heyday, 1850 to 1880, 11 breweries, most notably Rheingold, Piels and Schaefer, lined what was referred to as Brewers' Row. By the 1960s, however, Bushwick was profoundly different, beset by crime and poverty and all the abject social conditions that they bring – drug use, substandard schools, hunger and children born out of wedlock.

The demographics of this two-square mile neighborhood had also changed. Italian immigrants had replaced the Germans as the dominant group after World War I. Then blacks, including Stryker's parents, moved to Bushwick from the south after World War II, followed by Puerto Ricans from the island commonwealth.

In turn, whites fled, many fearful of the message shouted loud and clear by unscrupulous real-estate agents.

"Don't wait until it's too late," read one common flyer stuffed into mailboxes.

In person, agents were even blunter: "Sell while you can."

And sell they did.

To make matters worse, sleazy speculators were among the buyers, paying about $8,000 per home, then selling them to blacks and Puerto Ricans eager for a piece of the American Dream. They took advantage of a federal mortgage program that helped achieve that dream for an average price of $20,000. It was a price many new families really couldn't afford. So when they defaulted, the homes fell vacant.

Many of the empty homes were then torched by owners so they could collect on their insurance. Others were set afire by gangs or mischievous teens, though they too had dollars signs in mind, swooping in after firefighters left and stealing copper wiring and other fixtures that could be sold to scrap dealers.

Destruction came easy, as many of them were wooden row houses with cocklofts – the space that lies between the top apartment and roof and is connected through rows of buildings. A fire in one building in seconds became a fire in several buildings, or a half dozen, and often more. Picture water seeping into any open space. Now, imagine it as fire and you get the picture.

By 1972, about 500 buildings in Bushwick were vacant because of bad loans. Those untouched by arsonists were of no value to investors. Who, the thinking went, would invest in Bushwick? Those living there, however, had little choice. To survive, they coped. Worried parents, for instance, had their kids sleep in street clothes so they could make a quicker escape from a late-night fire. And some vigilant residents spent nights outside their homes, armed and ready to shoot if someone thought about setting fire to an abandoned building on the block.

City Hall tried to solve the problem. At one point, rental subsidies for welfare recipients were increased. Hopefully, the city figured, landlords would see that as an incentive to rent their apartments to those beneficiaries. They did, and by the mid-1970s half the 100,000 or so residents in Bushwick were on welfare. One such family gamed the system, collecting $40,000 in welfare benefits and replacement costs for 13 fires it set before being arrested, according to a newspaper report at the time.

Crime was also up across the city, especially in Bushwick, where robberies and burglaries soared as a sense of desperation set in. Some sections of the beleaguered neighborhood were so bad two patrol cars were sent to every 911 call. When the cops in one car got out to respond to the matter at hand, the cops in the second car would keep an eye on the empty patrol car.

By 1975, America was still two years away from a shocking visual – a burning Bronx building caught on camera during the World Series. In Brooklyn, Bushwick was already on fire.

To Stryker, however, Bushwick was home. Stevie was born in December 1966 to Ruby and the Reverend Ezekiel Stryker. Stevie's father grew up in Atmore, Alabama, settled into a 6-foot-1 inch frame and became a fire-and-brimstone Pentecostal minister. Bushwick, in many ways, struck him as a sinner's paradise. His son, he vowed, would not sin. When he spoke, he made sure little Stevie listened.

"If he said to shut off the TV you just knew," Stryker remembered. "You did it. There was no arguing."

If the Reverend Stryker had a back story, little Stevie never heard much about it, such was his father's old-school ways. Even so, some moments, as vague and general as they were, still stick with the son today. Dad's father, he later learned from relatives, was the victim of a race murder in Alabama. Dad had married once before and lost his wife and six of his eight children in a horrific car crash, also in Alabama. It's memorialized in a newspaper story that printed a United Press International dispatch from Bethel Springs, Tennessee.

Stevie's mother, Ruby, also hailed from Alabama – Luverne, a dot on the map that today has a population of 2,800 and describes itself as the "Friendliest City in the South." Born in 1921, Ruby, one of 23 children, knew it much differently as a bi-racial child routinely mocked and rejected by both blacks and whites. Still, she persevered, picking cotton at the farm where she was raised.

In high school, Ruby was known as "Spider" for her prowess as the point guard on an otherwise all-white girls' basketball team. But her real talents, dancing and jazz singing, inspired her to pursue a career as an entertainer. Her mother felt otherwise, so much so that when she found out Ruby was heading to New Orleans to chase her dream she yanked her off a train, took her back home and made sure she spent her free time in church.

As a young woman she became an evangelist, perhaps the first such black woman to do so in Alabama, and devoted her life to spreading the word of the Lord.

It wasn't until the early 1960s that she migrated to New York and met the man she would marry. Together, they founded a house of worship, Bethel Temple Church, in Bushwick, and pursued a life of faith. The Reverend Stryker was the stoic, intimidating presence, his wife the clapping, swaying counterpart. His gospel to her jazz.

Then, at age 45 – and despite what doctors had told her – Ruby got pregnant and gave birth to her only child. Home for the Strykers was a house on Covert Street, near Bushwick Avenue. Every few minutes the rumbling of the train on the elevated subway tracks that run above bustling Broadway could be heard. The house had a stoop, a front gate, a backyard and the love and discipline any kid needed to thrive. It was, simply, home – safe, secured, structured. Stevie and his parents took the downstairs apartment. Upstairs lived his half-sister, Eleanor, her husband and their kids.

Bushwick in the late 1960s and 1970s was bad and getting worse, but Stevie was relatively shielded from that. His dad worked as a restaurant cook but devoted most of his other hours to the ministry. Indeed, church would shape little Stevie in ways he couldn't yet fathom as a boy. But in the early 1970s he was just another kid in Brooklyn.

"Bushwick – I loved it," he said with sincere affection. "Stickball, street football, basketball. A lot of fun. A lot of good times. My dad was well-known in the neighborhood. Everybody knew him as Reverend Stryker. My mom – she was the rock. She used to work as a seamstress, then she was home, raising me. I'd wake up in the morning and the mailman, Mr. John, would be in the kitchen eating breakfast, instead of delivering the mail. Things like that I remember clearly.

"But what I remember, more than anything, it was me, my dad and my mom, having dinner all the time together. That was a pet peeve of my dad's. He insisted on it, having dinner together all the time. I'd be in the living room, playing. I had a fascination for those little Army figures. And I loved my Rock 'Em Sock 'Em Robots. Then my dad would come home and it was all about sitting there together. 'Put those toys away and come to dinner.'"

Mostly, Stryker recalled, he would learn from his parents by watching and listening.

"Back then, you really didn't question your parents," he said. "My kids now will ask me, if they see me putting on my jacket, 'Hey dad, where you going? What are ya up to?' I would never question my dad. He'd leave and I'd knew he'd be coming back home. He was from the old school. If he were alive today I'd love to hear what he'd have to say about these time outs parents give their kids. Time out? It would be more like knock you out. He wasn't affectionate. He wasn't the talkative type. But every Easter I'd have a new outfit. And every Christmas he'd take me shopping on Delancey Street in Manhattan. He just wasn't affectionate – at all. But I knew how he felt. I knew he loved me."

Stevie was also learning, though he wouldn't know it until he himself was married, how to be a man, a husband and a father.

"I didn't see him and my mom argue. If they had a disagreement it was always off to the side. I love my dad for many reasons. I probably can't even count them. But the greatest reason why I love my dad is for how he treated my mom. If a man ever wants his kids to love him treat their mother right. I watched him – he treated my mother right. I learned from him. My wife has health issues. I help her get out of bed, get the kids off to school. I'm old school, with a lot of new school swagger, but I got the old school from him. He took the garbage out. He didn't think it was appropriate for a woman to take the garbage out. And if the doorbell rang, he'd get it. It wasn't, 'Ruby get the door.' And my mother knew – 'Zeke somebody's at the door.' And he'd get it."

Stevie attended Public School 26 and Junior High School 296. A solid 'A' student – if he brought home a 'C' there'd be a lot of explaining to do – Stevie toed the straight and narrow. But Bushwick being Bushwick, it was difficult to avoid seeing what his father spent his life preaching against. The first time little Stevie saw the bad in people it shocked him. The incident is still fresh in his mind.

"I remember as a little boy seeing these guys, whenever the delivery trucks pulled up to the grocery stores, they would wait for the driver to take the stuff out and head inside the store," Stryker said. "Then they'd just pop the lock, snatch everything. Later, you'd see them coming through the neighborhood – 'I got bread. I got juice.' To this day I remember that.

"In the summer, when cars would be at a red light, I would see guys reach into cars and just snatch a lady's pocketbook. They'd pretend to be crossing the street like anyone else, then they'd just grab the bag and run. The first time I saw that, I was like, 'Wow! What is going on?' I remember there was a killing on the corner at a numbers spot. I lived in a tough neighborhood, but I always felt safe because of my parents. We'd drive around, me and my dad, and he'd point to certain guys and say, 'Stay away from them. They're selling that stuff.'"

That stuff – cocaine and heroin in particular – was all over Bushwick. Dealers controlled the building on Stevie's corner and they seemed to have a stranglehold on the homes next to his and across the street. Stevie was never tempted. And only the good Lord knows what his father would have done to him had he strayed. Besides, there was little time to be tempted. Home by six every night for dinner. No exceptions.

And the dealers, for their part, didn't bother little Stevie. They, too, were afraid of his father to pull such a stunt.

"If those guys were smoking cigarettes and saw my dad, they'd put them out. 'Hello, Reverend Stryker. Hello, Mrs. Stryker.' We would walk to church and see that nonsense going on and I remember saying to myself, 'I would love to get them off the street.' As I look back, I guess that was my motivation for becoming a cop."

By 1975, New York City was begging the federal government for financial assistance as it teetered on the edge of bankruptcy. Outside the city, no one cared, such was the way the city was viewed beyond the Hudson River. The Big Apple has always lured dreamers from all corners of the world – actors from Alabama, doctors from Des Moines, engineers from Egypt. Name the place, the people there wanted to be here. At the same time, however, there was little sympathy, at least in official circles, for a city seen by many as arrogant, elitist, boastful and in desperate need of an attitude adjustment.

When then-President Gerald Ford denied New York City the financial aid it sought the *New York Daily News* blasted him in a front-page headline on October 30th, 1975.

"Ford to City: Drop Dead."

He never actually uttered those words, but the sentiment was all the same.

Nonetheless, the president two months later signed legislation granting the city federal loans. But the damage was done. The headline, Ford later said, cost him dearly when he ran for president against Jimmy Carter. The loans, meanwhile, eventually helped the city right its financial course. But it took some time, and the city was far from out of the woods.

Then, on July 29th, 1976, a man walked up to an Oldsmobile parked on a Bronx street and opened fire. The first shot struck 18-year-old Donna Lauria as she was getting out of the car. She fell to the ground, dead.

The next shot struck her friend, Jody Valenti, 19, who was still sitting in the car. The bullet struck her thigh, but she survived. The mystery gunman then turned and walked away. Before the city would learn his real name he was simply the .44-Caliber Killer, for his gun of choice.

Then he became even more mystifying.

"I am the Son of Sam," he said in a note left at another Bronx crime scene, a double murder. "I love to hunt. Prowling the streets looking for fair game – tasty meat. The women of Queens are the prettyest."

The mystery man was clearly not a good speller, but he was good at capturing the city's attention and scaring the living hell out of many New Yorkers.

By June of 1977 New Yorkers were most obsessed with two things: the New York Yankees, a rollicking collection of superstars and personalities who were on their way to a World Series title, and the NYPD's relentless pursuit of the Son of Sam.

The second letter, in the same month, was sent to *New York Daily News* columnist Jimmy Breslin.

"Hello from the gutters of N.Y.C.," the killer wrote, "which are filled with dog manure, vomit, stale wine, urine and blood. Don't think that because you haven't heard from me in a while that I went to sleep."

A task force of some 300 cops worked day and night trying to identify the Son of Sam. Not yet 11 years old, little Stevie had a singular thought as school let out for the summer: could the Son of Sam be coming to Bushwick? No matter that the killer appeared to prefer white women with brunette hair. When you're a kid fear tends to trump reason.

Then, on the night of July 13th, lightning struck several power lines north of the city, tripping its circuit breakers. Just past 9:30 p.m., New York City was plunged into darkness. Twelve years earlier, during the previous blackout, there were a handful or riots and some looting. For the most part, though, New Yorkers were calm, quiet and peaceful, sharing flashlights and generally coming together to weather the crisis. This time, in the moneyed sections of Manhattan, at least, it was much the same. Tony restaurants, for instance, moved their tables outside so their well-heeled patrons could dine al fresco. And at the Winter Garden Theater on Broadway the cast members of "Beatlemania" led the audience in a sing-along of Beatles hit songs.

But on the other Broadway, in Bushwick, all hell broke loose. Looters ran wild, carrying whatever they could handle – clothing, boxes of diapers, steaks, television sets and even couches. In many cases, after a store had been plucked clean of every last piece of merchandise, someone simply set it afire.

Over the next three days, the Fire Department fought 1,037 blazes. Poor neighborhoods everywhere were scarred but none more so than Bushwick. Despite its proximity to the gleaming lights of Manhattan, Bushwick already felt like a third-world country. It had the highest infant mortality rate in the city, 40 percent of its roughly 100,000 residents were on public assistance and about 80 percent – 80 percent! – didn't have a job. After the smoke cleared, it looked even worse.

"I remember being scared," Stryker said. "I was 10 years old. I sat with my mom in the living room with a flashlight listening to a battery-operated radio. In my mind, I'm thinking the Son of Sam is gonna kill more people because there's a blackout. I remember my mom and I having a conversation and she said, 'Don't worry about that. Everything's gonna be OK.'"

Bushwick, indeed, appeared safe from a serial killer but not from its own residents.

"I remember my dad going to church to check to make sure everything was OK. There was this bike shop on the corner – Joe's Bike Shop – and I remember them tearing the gates down during the looting."

The rioting eventually subsided. The Son of Sam did not.

On July 21st, on the opposite end of Brooklyn, in the shadow of the Verrazano Bridge, he approached a parked car and opened fire on Stacy Moskowitz and Robert Violante, both 20 years old and on their first date. Moskowitz died 18 hours later. Violante was blinded.

Sam's reign of terror would eventually end a month later when police tracked a parking summons placed on a car windshield near where Moskowitz and Violante were shot. The car belonged to one David Berkowitz. That day, and for the rest of the city's most tumultuous summer, New Yorkers breathed a sigh of relief as Berkowitz was paraded before the media in handcuffs, no longer free to kill. But to a little kid in Bushwick the world outside his front door was now a much different place.

###########

"Time for church."

Stevie would have preferred root canal without anesthesia. Or perhaps a swift kick to the groin. Either, he said, would have been a better option than hearing those words. But when you're the son of a Pentecostal minister the church is your home away from home. Today, it's the guiding force in his life. Back then, it was one big pain in the ass.

"I was there all the time," he remembered. "Bible study on Wednesday night. Services on Friday. Sundays, of course. On Saturday nights my father would be there giving out fish dinners. And I'd always have to help out. Man, there were times I just didn't want to go. But I had to be there."

For the Reverend Stryker, of course, the ministry was like oxygen, and despite his hard exterior he was a good and decent man. Too good, his son believed, too decent. Too often, he'd bail out of jail the troublemaking kid of a poor parishioner. It didn't come for free, of course. He would sit the young offender down in his living room, admonish him for the grief he'd just caused his parents, then warn him about staying out of trouble. To Stevie, it was obvious dad's speech was going in one ear and out the other one.

Was he too cynical for his age? Maybe. But it was clear he more and more was at odds with his father's way of doing things. Fortunately, the rebellion didn't show when it came time to study. Stevie attended Forest Hills High School, in Queens. His father drove him every morning to save Stevie a lengthy bus and subway trip. And along the way he was reminded what needed to be done.

"There was no debate, no settling for low grades. I had to do well."

But by Stevie's senior year in high school he had just about had enough of his father's methods. Too square. Too strict. Too up his ass about every little thing. Becoming a lawyer was still a vague notion he had. Becoming a cop? Not even on his radar at that point. He had been accepted to North Carolina Agricultural and Technical State University – one of the nation's top black schools – and, as far as his parents were concerned, that's where Stevie was headed.

Enter Raymond Sanchez.

"One day I'm home and my friend Raymond Sanchez rings the doorbell – 'Stevie, I gotta go down to the Marine Corps recruitment station.' I said, 'OK.' So I went down there with him and signed up."

Just like that. Almost on a whim.

Sanchez failed his physical at the Fort Hamilton Army Base because he had asthma. But Stevie passed. The decision, to say the least, was not met warmly on Covert Street. Stevie, not yet trained to fight like a Marine, was ill-prepared for the beating he feared he would receive from his physically imposing father. That fear never materialized. What he got was much worse.

"The day the recruiter came to pick me up to take me to boot camp my dad stayed in his room," Stryker said. "My mother had to sign the papers. They both didn't want me to go, but my mother knew I wanted to go. I got up about 3:30 to get my stuff ready. My mother is sitting in my room – I'm her baby – and she tells me, 'Your dad will be all right.'

"The recruiter comes about 5:30, he honks the horn, I grab my stuff and I hug my mom. I want to see my dad. He's in bed, he's got his back to the door, but I know he's up. I say, 'All right, dad. I'm leaving now. I'll see you soon.' No response. I go downstairs. I leave, and when I look back my mother is in the doorway, waving goodbye.

"My father never got out of bed."

CHAPTER 3 – JOINING THE MARINES

Stevie Stryker wanted so badly to be a Marine, he actually scammed his way into service.

Stryker, all 5 feet 7 inches of him, is middle-aged now and looks like many things. Accountant comes to mind. Office manager. Concert pianist, maybe.

Cop does not come to mind.

And certainly not United States Marine.

Not now. And most definitely not then, at age 17, just a few months removed from high school. The sergeant during baby-faced Stevie's physical in Brooklyn certainly thought that.

Stevie had the previous month weighed in at 110 pounds – a full 10 pounds below the minimum standard. He had to put on the weight, he was told, or forget about a gig with the Marines.

No problem, his mother told him, stuffing him every day with steak, eggs, French fries, anything to stick to his bones.

Stevie felt heavier. But was he heavy enough?

On weigh-in day, he stepped onto the scale. The sergeant looked at him skeptically. Stevie stared back, trying to look tough but knowing full well he might not qualify.

The sergeant peered at the scale: 117 pounds.

"You really want to be a United States Marine?"

"Yes, sir."

"Well, I don't have the right to stop someone from being a Marine."

With that, the sergeant slid the scale indicator from left to right, from 117 to 120.

"He looked at me and said, 'Oorah, Marine,'" Stryker recalled. "I was in."

Next stop: Parris Island.

In 1562, a French explorer, Jean Ribault, led a group that tried to colonize Parris Island, in what is now South Carolina. The group built an outpost, Charlesfort, but full colonization never materialized. Eventually, the English took control of the area and the island was divided into a number of plantations growing indigo, then cotton. During the Civil War, then afterwards, freed slaves called Parris Island home.

In 1861, after Union forces captured Port Royal Sound, in which Parris Island is located, the island became a coaling station for the U.S. Navy. The Marines were first stationed on Parris Island in 1891. In 1915, it was officially named a Marines training site. Its address is 283 Blvd De France, Parris Island, SC 29905. Do not be fooled. The only France on Parris Island is the address, and there is certainly no Paris there. No quaint cafés. No stylish European women dressed in black. No three-hour lunches. No midday strolls. It is 8,095 acres of torture.

"Boot camp was three months of hell," Stryker said. "You couldn't pay me to go back."

The day after your first day in boot camp is sort of like the day after you thought it'd be a great idea to have a red dragon tattooed on your neck. That is, not such a good idea. Stryker certainly felt that way, but his upbringing set him apart, enabled him to get through the day, then the next, and so on. All despite a drill sergeant like no other.

A Marine drill sergeant will know a recruit better than his mother does. He'll know who the posers are and who the stars are. He'll know, and know fairly quickly, which ones will be sent home, which ones will quit and which ones will be a success, there and in life. The problem, however, is the drill sergeant will treat you like shit no matter his opinion of you – even if he sees greatness. If anybody could be a Marine then it wouldn't be the Marines. And so, the recruits, even the best of them, typically end each day praying for the end of time.

"There are only two ways off this island, maggots – a pine box or a Greyhound bus," Stryker's drill sergeant was fond of saying. "Stryker, did your mamma make a mistake and put you on the wrong bus? Shouldn't you be on that little school bus? How did you get into my corps?"

"I get it," Stryker would say to himself. "He's trying to make me tougher, trying to see if I'll crack. I'm not gonna crack. I'll slough it off, meet your angry questions with a straight answer. Maybe even smile."

Oh, no.

"On picture day, I made the mistake of smiling," Stryker said. "The drill sergeant, he gets in my face – 'Stryker, Marines don't smile. When we go to take these pictures if I see you with a smile on your face, I'm gonna kill you.'

"I swear to you, at that moment, I believed him. So for a while, every day, the sergeant would come out every morning, tell a joke, stand in my face and say, 'Everyone can laugh, except Stryker.' If I laughed I had to do pushups – and there were some days where that happened.

"Another time, during combat drills, the guy I was up against hit me in the helmet and I fell off the stage. I was embarrassed, about ready to bawl. The sergeant's like, 'Dry them tears up. I don't care what you do, but you get back up there and don't let that happen again.' The guy did the same move, tried to fake me out, but this time I didn't go for it and I hit him in the balls. I got disqualified, but when I walked off my drill instructor winked at me."

As boy was becoming man, Ruby Stryker was back home wondering why her only child wasn't writing her as often as he had initially been. Truth be told, Stryker certainly missed home and he wasn't too old to be a mama's boy. But his unit had been living in the field and there just hadn't been enough time for calls home.

Stryker's dad begged to differ. One morning, Stryker found himself in the gunnery sergeant's office. Despite his size, his kid looks and the utter joy his superiors took in trying to break him down, Stryker was well on his way to graduating with a stripe on his uniform. Private first class. That might have explained the sergeant's breezy mood on that day.

The phone was off the hook, receiver on the desk. The sergeant closed the door.

"Stryker, you must come from a good home."

"Yes, sir."

"I've never had parents call my boot camp and demand to speak to their child."

He grabbed the phone.

"I have on the phone Reverend Stryker and he wants to know why you haven't written your mama."

Stryker wanted to find the nearest patch of dirt, dig a hole and climb into it. At the same time, he knew this was his father's way of showing he cared.

Screenwriters are told never write "on the nose," meaning never have your character say exactly how he or she feels. Instead, the character should do or say something else that conveys the same meaning.

This was Reverend Stryker's way of showing his true feelings. Never say what you mean. Show it through your actions. Stryker took the phone and accepted his father's verbal tongue lashing. The sergeant, remarkably, was not angry, and Stryker moved on, graduating near the top of his class. His parents did not attend the ceremony. Stryker was not surprised, but when he flew back to New York City his father was there to pick him up at LaGuardia Airport.

By then, Stryker was a changed man – purposeful, confident and ready for life. Still, he was back in Brooklyn, filled with just enough machismo for one to worry: Is he going to do something stupid, something he'll regret for the rest of his life?

That nearly happened.

One warm night, he, Raymond Sanchez and another friend, Marcus, went to a block party near the Stryker home. There was food. There were pretty girls. And there was at least one other guy there who had an eye on the gold initials hanging from the gold chain around Stryker's neck.

Stryker knew the guy, went to junior high school with him, sat next to him in math class. But that innocent kid was long gone, replaced by a guy hooked on crack and walking the streets with a new name, Unique.

"I saw this guy at the party and I spoke to him," Stryker said. "But he just smirked when I said, 'What's up?' Didn't recognize me. Didn't remember me."

After the party, as Stryker, Raymond and Marcus were walking home, there was Unique, with a small crew of his friends, eyeballing Stryker's jewelry.

"Give me that chain," someone in the crew said.

Instinctively, Stryker took a step back, prepared to fight. Unique had something else in mind. He pulled out a black handgun and pointed it at Stryker's face while one of his buddies reached over, grabbed Stryker's chain and snatched it right off his neck.

So much for hand-to-hand combat.

Unique and company ran off. Stryker and his friends took a deep breath, then Stryker made a beeline for his house, slipped into his parents' bedroom, found his father's jacket, reached into a pocket and pulled out a silver handgun.

The provenance of that gun spoke to the random nature of life, or at least life in Bushwick back then. One night some years earlier, there was a rustling in the backyard of the Stryker home. It sounded like someone trying to break in. And, indeed, that's exactly what it was, a 20-something young man looking for a quick score. Then suddenly, with Stryker's dad hustling to see what was going on and his only child, not quite a teen, racing to his bedroom window for a look, the would-be thief turned tail, scaled the fence and ran away.

The next day, Stevie and a bunch of other kids were hanging out in the backyard.

One friend, Russell, saw the gun, picked it up and nearly gave the Reverend Stryker a heart attack.

"Hey, whose toy is this?" Russell wondered.

The reverend knew it was no toy but rather a revolver that the would-be thief apparently dropped the night before.

All of a sudden, the Strykers had a gun in their house.

"It's just the way things were in Bushwick," Stryker said. "My father didn't get rid of the gun – and I knew where he kept it."

Almost as if on cue, the Reverend Stryker was soon put to the test.

His wife took their son clothes shopping on Good Friday.

Stryker remembered walking down Broadway, proud owner of a brand new Easter suit, a blue pinstripe number, with a light blue tie. To top it off, they stopped at Buster Brown for a pair of impossibly shiny black shoes.

"My mom was holding my hand with her right hand and holding the two bags in her left hand," Stryker remembered. "All of a sudden, I felt a hard pull. A man ran by and snatched the bags right out of my mother's hand. We almost fell, and I remember seeing this tall guy running down Broadway. My mom wanted to know if I was OK. I was, but I remember crying more because I was scared than anything else."

Mother and son walked home. Dad found out what happened, went upstairs, then returned a few minutes later, fully dressed, the newfound gun tucked in his waistband.

"What was he wearing?" dad wanted to know.

"It happened so fast," mom said. "I just don't remember."

No matter. The Reverend Stryker, man of God, went cruising up and down Broadway, packing heat.

"He didn't find him," Stryker said. "But when he came home later that evening I was too scared to talk to him about it.

"He took me out the next day to buy another suit for Easter."

Now, fresh out of the Marines, Stryker, at least as he exhibited during boot camp, was not the kind of man to give in to base instinct, to let others drag him down to their level.

Suddenly, though, there he was, racing out of his home, gun in hand. Just like his father had.

"Where'd you get that gun?" a stunned Raymond wanted to know.

"I found it."

Stryker wasn't lying.

"Now, where is he?"

Unique, however, would live to see another day. He and his crew – fortunately for them, and for Stryker – were nowhere to be found.

"One hundred percent, I would have shot him," Stryker said. "The adrenaline was pumping. You got that bull's swagger going on. No doubt in my mind if I had seen him I would have shot him."

Some days later, Stryker's dad tore their home apart, "looking for something important," he told his son. Drawers pulled upon, closets emptied. All to no avail.

That something, the gun, was long gone. Stryker had the morning after getting robbed given the gun to another friend, Andre, who was having some problems of his own with a young buck from the neighborhood and felt he needed it for protection. Andre never got to use it, but in a cruel twist he was later robbed and shot, confined the rest of his life to a wheelchair. The culprit was not the guy with whom he had been at war but rather, at least according to strong street talk, Unique himself.

But street talk doesn't hold up in a court of law, so Unique, or whomever did shoot Andre, got away with it.

Andre moved on and made a life for himself, working as a token booth clerk. Unique wasn't as lucky. His days of living hard eventually caught up with him when he was shot dead in the neighborhood.

The Marines, meanwhile, weren't quite yet done with Stryker.

Combat was still a possibility, with President Ronald Reagan worried about the growing Middle East tensions involving Libyan President Muammar el-Qaddafi and his potential plans to attack Israel, maybe even with nuclear weapons.

Stryker would eventually serve two more tours, but not in the battlefield. Instead, his recruitment officer saw Stryker for what he was – a charismatic young man as persuasive as he was charming. A lot of teens and men in their early 20s didn't need to be sold on the Marines. Even fewer did once Stryker got their ear. As a recruiter, Stryker realized perhaps his strongest asset – he knew how to talk to people, how to make an impression on them, how to convince them that what he was selling was the best thing for them. Stryker, if he believed in something, could make anyone else a true believer. The students he spoke to at local high schools and elsewhere quickly learned that.

"I basically told them why the Marines would be good for them, the same way they were good for me."

After three months of recruiting, however, it was off to Camp Lejeune, North Carolina, for another two years, first in a field support unit, then in a MAU, or Marine Amphibious Unit, a small air-ground task force trained to spring into action at a moment's notice.

Without realizing it, Stryker was honing skills that would later come in handy in some of the toughest neighborhoods in America. His mother, however, was home arranging for her only child to attend York College, in Jamaica, Queens. But even when he finished his military service and started college Stryker was still a work in progress, not quite sure what the next step would be.

While at York, a small institution that is part of City University of New York, Stryker surprisingly developed a taste for politics.

"I felt I had an ability to draw people," he said. "To talk to people."

But it was a loose, general affinity for a career to which he hadn't previously given much thought. At the same time, becoming a chef – watching his father cook had rubbed off on him – also seemed a possibility.

In other words, he wasn't quite sure what to do with himself and figured his future would very likely be determined by whatever next happened his way.

As a freshman, Stryker met a girl named Pam. She, too, would eventually become a cop, but at the time her mother was a branch manager for Independence Savings Bank. Stryker needed a job. Her mother gave him one, working at a branch in Brooklyn.

It was a part-time gig – $200 a week working first as a teller then later in customer service. The branch, one of those elaborate high-ceiling beauties, was close enough to home. Still, the father was there most nights to pick up his son. He was still a man of few words, but as always, his actions did the talking.

It wasn't long before Stryker's military training would come in handy – and it nearly cost him his job. One afternoon, as the bank was closing for the day, a young hothead tried to force his way past Nat, the 70-something security guard who was locking the front door. He was insistent and said he needed to make a transaction. The guard, long past his physical prime, kindly asked the man to come back tomorrow. But the guy had other ideas and forced his way in, Nat falling to the ground and catching Stryker's attention in the process.

"I hopped over the counter and confronted the customer – this was in the middle of the bank," Stryker said. "We exchange looks, and everybody was watching. Tense. Very tense."

Cooler heads prevailed, but the hothead got his way, "to my disgust," Stryker said, and was allowed to do what he had to do and be on his way.

The drama was far from over, however. The branch vice president of operations wanted Stryker fired, but he had the branch manager and the bank president in his corner. They went to bat for Stryker and saved his job.

"The president liked me because every day I would always say hello to him. 'Good morning, sir. How are you, sir?'" Stryker said. "I told him I was just defending Nat and that my Marine Corps training just kicked in and I wanted to stop him from attacking anyone else."

Impressed, the president moved Stryker to customer relations, a natural fit. There was one condition, however: the branch manager made sure Stryker's desk was next to hers. There would be no more mano a mano confrontations with the customers. At about that time, Stryker met Teri, a friend of a regular bank customer with whom he was friends. He and Teri dated and would eventually have a child together – Erica,* born in May 1989.

Teri and Stryker would fall in and out of love before eventually calling it quits in 1994. For years his relationship with Erica was strained and erratic. It was Stryker's first real personal adult crisis. He could have handled it better, but he and his daughter would eventually find the best in each other and work things out, though it would take some years to do so.

Before Erica's birth, Teri had made a suggestion that would change his life: take the city's civil service exam. It was a perfectly reasonable suggestion that would allow Stryker a chance to make decent money and take advantage of his military service. He'd get extra points on the test for having served in the Marines. And, he figured, who better to become a cop than a soldier? He cut short his college education five credits shy of an associate's degree. What he couldn't have known at the time was he had just found his life's calling.

CHAPTER 4 – NYPD BLUE

Stryker's official start date as a cop was June 30th, 1992.

Today, the NYPD is bigger than many American cities, but back then, there were three city police departments – the vaunted NYPD, the Housing Police Department and the Transit Police Department.

Cops from Housing had one of the toughest jobs in town, patrolling more than 300 city-run developments, many of which were veritable crime havens, with too many of its residents living in fear. Their brethren in Transit patrolled the nation's largest subway system.

The city was still three years away from merging all three departments into one, so most recruits, when asked which department they wanted to join, said the NYPD, the gold standard for American policing. Checking that on the application wasn't a guarantee you'd get in, but most did it anyway.

Stryker went the other way, picking Transit.

If Housing was the unwanted, red-headed stepchild, Transit was only slightly more desirable. It was far from an easy or cushy gig. Still, most New Yorkers didn't consider Transit officers real cops, and "Big Brother," as some doing subway duty sometimes called the NYPD, was always looking down its nose at them.

"You worked in the hole, you breathed too much steel dust, you didn't know your way above ground," Stryker said. "All the jokes, the putdowns. I heard 'em all. But Bill Bratton had turned things around there."

Bratton, a rising star in law enforcement, had two years earlier been named to replace outgoing Transit Chief Vincent Del Castillo following a record bad year in subway crime – 16,906 felonies in 1989, an 18 percent increase over the total for 1988. Bratton came from Boston, where since 1986 he had been superintendent of the Metropolitan Police Department. His hiring in New York City could not have come at a worse time for the city's subway system. Crime was out of control, the department's decoy unit had been publicly accused of making false arrests, morale was low and union leaders were pushing for a merger with the NYPD, a move Transit officials vehemently opposed. Bratton was among them, saying at the time that "transit work requires a high degree of specialization and training that could be lost in such a move."

It didn't much matter. Bratton didn't last long, leaving in January 1992, shortly before Stryker joined the force, to take the No. 2 job in the Boston Police Department.

But he had left behind a department far different than the one he had inherited. It was more proactive, and various innovative management strategies helped spark a double-digit drop in subway crime. That, in turn, sent morale among its officers soaring. For one young would-be officer, what stood out most was Bratton's boldest decision.

"They had Bratton, they had new vests, they had all this publicity," Stryker said. "But the Glock 9mm – that's all I saw. That's what made the difference. It was a real gun, a solid gun. I was in the Marines so I was used to carrying a gun like that. I figured that if I'm going to go in the street I didn't want a damn .38. I wanted the 9mm. It looked more impressive, too. I remember going to an event where there were representatives from the three departments. The guy from Transit had the 9mm and he looked sharp."

Standard now, the 9mm at the time was viewed warily by many law enforcement officials because it held 16 bullets, compared to the traditional six-shot .38-caliber revolver. There was concern that thick crowds, both above and below ground, made it more likely a bystander would be hit, either directly or by a bullet ricocheting off a train or the station's infrastructure. The 9mm was also more likely to jam. Bratton saw past that, saw the disadvantage cops were at compared to criminals armed to the teeth and made the 9mm the standard Transit weapon.

"That's what did it for me," Stryker said.

############

When a New York City police officer is sworn in it is typically with much fanfare. A big ceremony at St. John's University, in Queens, for instance, or Madison Square Garden.

In 1992, however, then-Mayor David Dinkins pulled a fast one. In a move both criticized as the worst kind of fiscal chicanery and lauded as brilliant political gamesmanship, Dinkins ordered all 2,104 police recruits to begin their training on June 30th at 11:59:59 p.m., the last second of the fiscal year.

It was, a City Hall aide admitted proudly, "a gimmick with a capital G," a ploy that allowed the police class to start training in the 1991-1992 fiscal year, as required by state law. That allowed the city to defer pension contributions for the recruits into the 1993-1994 fiscal year because the budget for the 1992-1993 fiscal year had already been approved.

The move was Dinkins' way of pushing back against the state Legislature, which wanted greater control of Safe Streets, Safe City, a popular public safety initiative, and had accused the mayor of using funds for the program to plug the budget gap and not moving quickly enough to hire new police officers.

Because the salary for one second of work by a police recruit was four-tenths of one cent, standard fiscal practice allowed that salary to be rounded down to zero. That meant the recruits got no salary for that one second, allowing the city to avoid pension contributions for the 1991-1992 fiscal year and – since the already approved budget didn't include pension spending for new cops – for the 1992-1993 fiscal year, thus saving the city $20 million.

None of this meant a hill of beans to the new recruits. Hell, most policy wonks had a hard time figuring out what Dinkins had just done. All Stryker knew was that he was required to show up at Brooklyn Technical High School for an (almost) midnight swearing in.

"Half of us were falling asleep," Stryker said. "But they did it quick. It was like, 'OK, now you're a cop – now go home, get some sleep and see you tomorrow.'"

The Police Academy proved to be quite a run for Stryker. His military experience gave him a leg up on many of the other young officers, most of whom were raw, immature and lacking in serious life experiences.

There's a reason young cops have traditionally been paired with veteran officers once they hit the streets. They don't know what they're doing. But Stryker was in full stride even while in the academy and was unafraid to voice his opinion, sometimes to his detriment. He got chewed out for slowing down during a training run and encouraging a female recruit who was out of shape and falling behind. The instructor gave Stryker a stern rebuke.

"Sir, I'm a Marine," Stryker explained. "A Marine doesn't leave anyone behind."

Some of the recruits were amused. But Stryker wasn't looking for laughs. No matter. The instructor felt Stryker was showing him up and told him so.

When the six months of academy training ended, it was onto three weeks of Transit training, then, all of a sudden, Stryker was a police officer ready for action.

But just like that his career nearly ended before it had a chance to get started.

During his first two weeks of field training he needed a screwdriver to adjust his radio. No screwdriver around, so Stryker picked up a knife.

Bad idea.

Stryker cut deeply into his finger, his trigger finger no less. The cut looked bad and there was blood everywhere, but he got stitched up and fully recovered, the everlasting scar a reminder of his rookie mistake.

Transit Chief Michael O'Connor had replaced Bratton, and morale was still high. In uniform, Stryker looked like a shiny penny and was brimming with confidence.

He quickly learned, however, that what they taught in the academy didn't necessarily apply on the streets or in the subway system.

One seemingly innocuous incident brought him endless ribbing, for years. Assigned to the Lexington Avenue line, he and his partner, Officer Owen Stowe, stepped onto a No. 6 train in Manhattan. It was typically crowded, with everyone doing their own thing, reading the paper or a novel, staring into space, looking at the subway map. Into this ordinary setting stepped, er, rolled, a panhandler in his 40s. He may have been down on his luck, but he was all muscle, built like a brick shithouse, as the saying goes.

But he had no legs.

And he was on a skateboard.

He saw the uniformed cops, glanced at their nameplates and smiled.

"Good evening, officers. I'm just trying to make some change, Officer Stryker."

"Now, I'm a softie," Stryker said. "So I say, 'Go ahead – it's OK.'"

It wasn't.

Skateboard's first target was a middle-aged woman who wanted no part of his spiel. Her money was her money and it wasn't going in his hands.

"Bitch," he called her.

Stryker and Stowe, now at the other end of the car, heard it clearly.

The woman didn't back down.

"You know what?" she shot back. "You've got some nerve."

"Fuck you, bitch."

Now the woman was fully enraged.

"I go over there," Stryker said, "I apologize to the lady and I tell this guy he has to leave."

"I'm not getting off the train, Stryker."

Now what? Handcuff a legless guy? It's like beating up a girl.

"I give him another chance," Stryker said. "I tell him he's gotta get off the train and he's insisting that he's not gonna go. I grab him and I go, 'Let's get off the train.' And what does he do? He grabs the pole.

"With both hands."

The train pulled into the 59th Street station.

"Now, the people on the train know what's going on, but the people getting on? They see this and they're screaming at us – 'My God, look at what these cops are doing!'"

Stowe tried to pry the guy's fingers off the pole. Stryker yanked on the guy's arms. Strong as an ox, he was not budging. Finally, Stryker punched Skateboard in the face.

There was stunned disbelief all around.

And more yelling and screaming.

But it worked, at least for a moment. Skateboard screamed out in pain and grabbed his face with one hand. Stowe pulled the other hand off the pole, but the struggle continued.

Finally, the two cops took control. Just then, a female officer stepped onto the platform.

"You need a 10-85?" she asked. That's police radio code for back-up.

"No way!" Stryker yelled out.

"Can you imagine calling for a 10-85 for a guy with no legs?" Stryker said. "We'd never hear the end of it. No way we were gonna let that happen so we grab this guy under both arms and fling him off the train.

"It was like in slow motion. He went crashing to the platform."

But by then someone else had already called the cops. So 20 of them showed up. Skateboard, stunned but not hurt, wanted a piece of Stryker, affecting his best martial arts pose.

The silly had become the ridiculous.

Fortunately for all involved, a sergeant stepped in, told Skateboard to calm down then directed him to get lost and consider himself lucky he wasn't getting arrested.

This was before the age of the smartphone, Twitter and YouTube. Still, word spread like wildfire and Stryker was the butt of countless jokes. Most of them were off-color and politically incorrect, including messages that Handi Man had called, a reference to the "In Living Color" skit, popular at the time, that depicted comedian Damon Wayans as a drooling, handicapped superhero.

Sometimes, Stryker learned, you just couldn't be so nice.

The next time, he told himself, he wouldn't be.

Indeed, not long after that encounter, Stryker was outside a station on the No. 2 line when he came across another panhandler. And not just any beggar but one with unmitigated gall and absolutely no shame.

"I'm on top of the stairs and looking down when I see this guy, in a wheelchair," Stryker said. "He gets out of the chair, folds it and carries it up the stairs. Just like that. Like it was nothing. I said to him, 'Come over here,' and he walks over with this big smile on his face, ha, ha, ha – 'What's up boss?'"

The best police officers care deeply about what's right and what's wrong. But that doesn't always mean an arrest has to be made.

Sometimes, a cop will warn and admonish. Sometimes, showing a little anger is all it takes.

"You can walk," Stryker said.

"You know, officer, I gotta get my hustle on. Know what I'm sayin'?"

"Do you know how hard people work for their money?" Stryker asked him. "Do you? And here you are pulling this scam."

Wheelchair wasn't smiling any more. He was holding a Maxwell House coffee can, stuffed to the rim with coins and dollar bills. Thirty bucks, at least, maybe more.

"Give me that," Stryker said, grabbing the can from him and throwing it down a sewer on the corner. "If I ever catch you doing this again I'll beat you so you need a wheelchair – now get lost!"

Stryker won that battle. But tomorrow, he figured, Wheelchair would return somewhere else, pulling the same old scam.

Younger offenders, he figured, could still be rehabilitated, but sometimes it meant dishing out some embarrassment.

"I get on the train in Times Square, 42nd and 8th, during rush hour," Stryker said. "The train is crowded, but there's this one kid, no more than 15. He thinks he's a tough guy. He's lying across three seats. I walk over. 'You wanna put your feet down so people can sit down?'

"Nah, man," was the response. "I ain't finished."

Oh, really?

"I drag him off the train in a headlock. One passenger holds the door and another passenger grabs the kid's book bag and comes with me. I don't even give him a summons. I walk him upstairs, right into the command. My lieutenant is there.

"What you got, Stevie?"

"I got a tough guy here, Lou. And I'm having a bad day, Lou. The last thing I need is some punk kid telling me in front of a crowded train he ain't getting off the seat. You know what I did, Lou? I dragged his ass up here like a little bitch. I should have shot him, right?"

The kid was petrified.

The lieutenant played along, amused.

"You know what I should do?" Stryker continued. "I should put you in the cell back there with the guy looking for a date for the prison dance. You wanna go to the prison dance? There's no girls there."

The cell was empty, but the kid didn't know that.

"But you know what I'm gonna do, Lou?"

"What are you gonna do, Stevie?"

"I'm gonna call his mom."

"Good idea, Stevie."

By now the kid's head was spinning.

Stryker wanted his number.

"You're gonna call my mother? What kind of cop are you?"

"I'm a cop that cares. I'm gonna call your mother and I hope your mother whoops your ass when you get home."

Mom answered the phone. Stryker calmly explained what happened, then put the kid on the phone.

His mother gave him an earful.

Chastened, he hung up, then hung his head. On his way out the door, he thanked Stryker and shook his hand.

############

Stryker's first real brush with danger started with a chain snatch, a popular crime at the time, even as the city was finally beginning to right itself after years of soaring shootings, murders and other assorted mayhem.

Stryker and another officer were riding the No. 2 subway line in Brooklyn when they heard a scream for help. The cops chased the thief out of the station, then several blocks through the neighborhood. The suspect then tried but failed to hide under a car, hoping Stryker, his partner and the dozen or so other cops who had responded to the scene wouldn't see him.

As Stryker dragged the suspect out from under the car, there it was – a handgun tucked into his waistband.

"What if?" crossed his mind for the first time.

"We didn't know he had a gun," Stryker said. "No one said he had a gun. I wasn't even thinking that, but he could have pulled it on us while we were chasing him, while he was under the car. You never know what can happen."

Still, for his work that day Stryker received his first accolade – Cop of the Month, December.

A few weeks later, Stryker took off his uniform for the last time. He'd been recruited to work plainclothes, a coveted spot that typically led to bigger and better things. It wasn't unheard of to get plucked so soon out the academy for such an assignment. But it didn't happen often.

Stryker, though, felt he was ready.

"Actually, I knew I could do it – at least, that's how I felt."

CHAPTER 5 – LEARNING FAST

There they were, a group of six young men loitering near the token booth, pondering, debating, wondering.

Do we jump the turnstile? Will the token booth clerk chase us? Are the cops around?

"Let's do it."

"Nah, not worth it."

"C'mon. I'll go first."

"Hurry! Go!"

Jumping the turnstile.

It is, to the working man, to the honest, tax-paying citizen, about as infuriating a quality-of-life crime as there can be. Sipping a beer in public? Hey, who hasn't done that? Loud radio playing? Please. But "theft of service," as it is legally known? Now that pisses people off. I've got three kids and still pay my way. You're a punk wearing $100 sneakers and you can't afford a subway fare?

For cops, the issue was far less philosophical: you're breaking the law so you're getting arrested. Beyond that, though, was the "Broken Windows" theory of policing. Proponents, and Bratton was certainly one, believed that if police enforced quality-of-life violations such as urinating in public, drinking booze on a street corner or jumping a subway turnstile then they could create a sense of comfort, safety and order. These offenders, the theory went, were often armed with weapons or had outstanding warrants. Not everyone agreed with that school of thought back then and not everyone agrees now, but beginning with Bratton it has remained a staple of New York policing.

On that day, however, Stryker wasn't thinking about police theory or philosophy. He was young and gung ho, and while he and his sergeant lingered nearby, dressed down in street clothes so as to blend in, Stryker made a decision. If those guys weren't gonna bring the game to the police then the police were gonna bring it to them.

"Sarge," he said. "Watch this."

With that, he walked past the would-be fare beaters. Looked down the platform to his left. Looked down the platform to his right. Then jumped the turnstile and pretended to wait for the train. Seconds later, the hapless half-dozen followed suited and jumped the turnstile, beaming with pride. Stryker took out his shield. The wrongdoers turned to make a run for it and were surrounded by the sergeant and other cops.

"Damn!" one of them yelled. "Fuckin' busted."

###########

The NYPD probably trains its officers for more scenarios and possibilities than any other police force in the world. How to deal with domestic disputes. The emotionally disturbed. Fights between neighbors. 911 calls about a man with a gun. Trespassers. Protesters. A husband holding his wife hostage. A wild animal running through the streets. A depressed teen threatening to jump off a bridge. Its Patrol Guide is thick enough, if used as a weapon, to fracture your skull. And it only gets heavier as it is amended, again and again. And yet, the training is just a guide. It teaches cops the basics. Everything else, they kind of figure out as they go along, talking to people, asking them questions, suggesting, cajoling and, if all goes well, settling an issue peacefully and without drama.

Stryker had that gift, had it probably from the first time his father dragged him to church and forced him to listen as he mesmerized his congregants at Sunday Mass, talking comfortably and easily. No script. No teleprompter. No talking points. Just a man who understood the power of the spoken word.

"That's where I got it from," Stryker said. "My father had the gift of gab. I have the gift of gab. You can teach a lot of things to a cop in plainclothes or an undercover, but if you have something that comes to you naturally, that's a big, big help."

His supervisors had taken notice of his skills, especially his ability to change his approach, depending on the personality of the dealer. He was told that if he maintained his professionalism and didn't let his success go to his head he could go a long way in the department.

Stryker appreciated the compliment.

"I like talking to people," he said. "People like talking to me. Man, if you can get people to open up to you, to talk to you, you don't need a gun. You can talk your way into anything. You can talk your way out of anything."

############

"You see any cops?"

This time the question was from a guy on the No. 7 train.

Stryker and two fellow officers, Owen Stowe and Carl Wright, had moments before stepped from the Times Square subway platform and into the last car on the train. They sat there and waited the few minutes before it would pull out and head to Queens. They had chosen the last car for good reason: the legit straphangers, the savvier ones anyway, knew to avoid the last car because that's typically where most bad guys went.

"All the trouble starts on the last car," Stryker said. "It's like the back of the bus or the back of the classroom. On the train you're farthest away from the conductor, three, four cars. We know this because we hear things when we're out there in plainclothes."

Two guys, early 20s, stepped into the last car. They nodded at Stryker and his colleagues. Then they took a seat. Now, other straphangers – regular folk, not cops or bad guys – approached. They took one look inside and headed elsewhere.

"So now it's just the five of us and one of the guys said to me, 'Yo, you see a cop out there?'" Stryker said. "I peek out the door. Look around. Nah, man, nobody."

Sold.

With that, he turned to his buddy, pulled a silver handgun out of his waistband and handed it over.

"Take this," one of the guys said to the other. "I'm tired of holding it. You hold it."

Stryker's did his best not to appear fazed.

"I look at my guys," Stryker said. "Wright gets up and leaves – he's going to tell the conductor not to move the train. Owen stands in the doorway because if his foot is there the doors can't close."

Gun guy and his friend sensed something was up.

"I had stuck my head out so I could see Wright," Stryker said. "I see him talking to the conductor. These guys are getting nervous now. They know something's up. Now, Wright's walking back to us. I look at these two guys, then I turn away. I pull my chain out with the shield, then I grab my gun.

"Step out of the car! Step out of the car!"

The average Joes – or at least two guys never before arrested – might have pissed themselves. Not these two.

"They were laughing," Stryker said. "They were like, 'Oh, shit – we thought maybe the other guys were cops but not you.' They were laughing more than they were upset."

No offense taken. But as they were being handcuffed on the platform in full display of dozens of New Yorkers, Stryker had a simple lesson for the suspects.

"This could be you," Stryker told them. "No reason you can't be doing what we're doing. Just think about that. One day you're gonna wanna grow up, now you got a gun possession on your record. They're like, 'Yeah, yeah, you right, you right.'"

In one ear and out the other.

During most of Stryker's eight months in plainclothes he was paired with a white partner. Race in New York City has always been an issue, always a factor.

In politics.

In housing.

And certainly in the NYPD.

Today, the patrol force, the uniformed cops who respond to more than a million 911 calls each year, is "majority minority," more black, Hispanic and Asian than white.

Still, stereotypes die hard.

In 2006, Sean Bell, a 23-year-old black Queens resident, was shot to death by police, the end to a brief, complicated encounter involving a strip club, undercover cops and host of young minority men hopped up on booze, testosterone and machismo.

Two of Bell's friends, both minorities, later testified at a trial for the three detectives charged in the case that when they first saw a dark-skinned man approach them they assumed he was a carjacker. In fact, he was actually an undercover NYPD detective.

Less than three years later, Omar Edwards, a young black police officer who had just finished his shift and was not in uniform, made the fateful mistake of pulling his gun and chasing a man trying to break into his car. Four white officers who were on-duty witnessed the chase, saw the gun and ordered Edwards to drop it. Edwards, perhaps in an attempt to identify himself, turned toward his brothers in blue, gun still in hand, and was shot dead.

Each day the NYPD's internal message system spits out scores of announcements. Funeral information for long-retired officers. Promotion ceremony missives. Reminders about new initiatives. And on and on. Nothing perhaps is more important than the "color of the day" announcement that lets every cop know which color to look for if there is a suspicion that the person they're eyeballing could actually be one of them.

Of course, there's a pretty good chance on any given day, say an orange day, that the guy standing on the corner with a bulge in his waistband is indeed a criminal who just happened to be wearing orange. So, then what? Hesitate and the mayor's speaking at your funeral. Shoot too soon and you're reading through your indictment. As a young black man, Stryker, like all minority officers working out of uniform or taking off-duty action, was fully aware of those risks and fully briefed on how to avoid friendly fire. Bark out your tax code. Yell out you're "on the job" or some other term unique to the police universe. Drop the gun and thrust your hands in the air.

For Stryker, the issue of race – of being a black man who became a cop a decade before its remarkable diversification – was never too far from the surface.

Indeed, on the day he watched the men, both black, exchange a gun on the subway, race was everywhere. The straphangers who saw five black guys – the suspects and the cops – and sat elsewhere? It was clear what they were thinking. The suspects who didn't believe Stryker was a cop? Race may have played a role in their thinking as well. When Stryker pulled his gun and forced the suspects off the train? Lord only knows what the scores of witnesses thought. Back-up officers in uniform may have been saying the same thing, though Stryker and his partners had made sure to wear the color of the day and pull their shields out so that they were hanging around their necks.

Now, whether a simple article of clothing is going to dispel 200-plus years of thinking and pre-conceptions...

"When you're black and you're a cop, it's always there," Stryker said. "You thought about it, but it didn't weigh on my mind. You thought about it but it didn't stop me from doing what I needed to do. I was aggressive and I didn't have the time to think about all these things, but it was in the back of my mind. Being a black cop, we always say color of the day don't mean nothing. When you got your gun out, the color of the day don't mean nothing."

Still, when a fellow cop suggested Stryker go work in narcotics so he could take the fast track towards becoming a detective, Stryker was more than intrigued. It would involve all the dangers of plainclothes work – multiplied by 100.

He jumped in head first.

CHAPTER 6 – GIVE ME DRUGS

If being young meant feeling invincible, then Stryker certainly thought that. He looked the picture of perfect health. He had his family. He had a great job. He had a bright future. So when he suddenly had brief, uncontrollable bowel movements sparked by sharp, sharp pains he thought the problem would pass, that it was much ado about nothing.

"I started noticing blood in my stool," Stryker said. "I could not keep food in my stomach. I bought every over-the-counter medicine imaginable but nothing worked. I kept it from my wife, then one day she noticed blood drops on the floor in the bathroom.

"I told her I cut my leg."

Besides, he figured, narcotics was calling and he wasn't about to let anything get in the way of that. His career was taking off, though joining narcotics meant starting over in more ways than one.

Here's the first rule for working narcotics, he quickly learned: you don't know nothing about nothing.

"When you're in narcotics, it's like you're not even a cop anymore," Stryker said. "They tell you, 'Forget everything you know, every rule you learned in the academy.' Now, you gotta think more like a criminal because if you're working undercover you're the bad guy, or at least pretending to be one."

Indeed, going undercover means always having to be on your toes, scrambling, looking for a story, any story, that will buy you time and, hopefully, buy you the guns and drugs you're looking for. Adjust, change up, give a different name, lie, stretch the truth, even walk away. Just do not get shot.

There's no one template that applies to all scenarios. In that regard, narcotics and conventional police work, in the subways or the streets, are guided by the same principle: assess each situation and respond accordingly. Life experience – how you grew up, your ability to talk to others, the ease or difficulty with which you respond to controversy – often contributes to an officer's ability to excel. Stryker had a very good instructor. All those years watching his father preach, often without notes, had taught him more than he could imagine.

Nothing, of course, could duplicate a real-life drug buy. The tension, the suspicion, the introduction of a new player, the price haggling. No amount of instruction can fully prepare an undercover for a real-life encounter.

Narcotics training, however, came pretty close.

For Stryker, it was three weeks at a police facility based at the Brooklyn Army Terminal. Three weeks of learning all the lingo – coke, for instance, goes by flake, snow, blow, toot, and base, among others. Three weeks of learning about packaging. About pricing. About trends. But most of all, three weeks of learning how to do the job right – and come back in one piece.

"You learn a lot, but honestly, I think the course is too short," Stryker said. "You're trying to take a programmed cop and change him completely. You're programmed to talk like a cop, walk like a cop. Now you come into this academy and in three weeks you have to be deprogrammed. That's difficult. That's especially difficult for a guy who maybe didn't grow up in the streets. It may be a little different for someone like myself and others who grew up in it, in some of these rough neighborhoods.

"I think it gives a guy like myself a little bit of an advantage, as opposed to a white or black cop who grew up in the suburbs of Long Island. Now, I'm not saying it's a black or white thing because I knew white undercovers who were excellent and black undercovers who, you'd look at them and say, 'What the hell are you doing?'

"So I don't believe it's a black or white thing when it comes to being an undercover – it's a personality thing. It's a heart thing. It's a fearless thing. It's an ability to adapt."

The goal was simple: you're a cop working undercover and looking to score. The dealer, meanwhile, was looking to make money. But he also had his radar up, wondering if the buyer was really a cop.

But wait – the "dealer" in narcotics training was actually a cop. This was training, after all. How life-like can it really be?

"You'd be surprised," Stryker said. "First of all, you wanna do well. You know this is a test to see if they'll take you. And when you're in it your heart is pounding. You're sweating. You just wanna do it right."

One such "purchase" illustrated his point. Stryker was about to make a buy, but the dealer was suddenly skeptical.

"You a cop?"

"Me?" Stryker asked? "No fucking way?"

"Don't play me, yo. I seen you in my neighborhood talking to other cops."

"Fuck that. You must be talking 'bout my twin brother. He's a cop – and I hate cops. Maybe *you're* a cop."

Not bad, Stryker's sergeant told him. You seem to have a knack.

There were stumbles, of course, but mostly Stryker had a sense he had found his niche. He was quick to adapt, quick to react. If the "dealer" zigged, he zagged. If he threw a curveball, Stryker fouled it off, buying himself enough time to come up with a good answer. Or he simply hit it out of the park and made the "buy."

By the end of training, Stryker was still standing. He and maybe a half-dozen other undercovers out of an original class of about two dozen. Some dropped out the first day, clearly aware they weren't up to it. Others gave it a shot and ultimately decided this wasn't for them. Still others were told they'd be better off as investigators, not undercovers.

The day of Stryker's first actual buy on the streets?

Don't ask.

"They teach you that when you're walking up on the target, take notice of what the guy looks like – what's he wearing, is he fat or skinny, does he have a scar on his face? Is there something unusual about the guy that you can say out loud as you're walking away so it gets heard on the wire?"

Done right, the field team, which is typically far enough away so as to not be seen, can know who to grab when the supervisor hears the description.

So what happened?

Stryker, from here on in known to the NYPD as UC 2717, for Undercover 2717, was given an assignment – go make a buy on 119th Street, a notoriously easy spot to score.

As he approached the dealer he barked out a description of the seller. So far, so good, and when Stryker, 10 bucks in hand, said he wanted two vials of crack the dealer gave it up, no questions asked.

But then Stryker lost focus as he walked away, unable to describe what the dealer was wearing.

What if, he would later learn, the guy he initially described turned out not to be the guy who sold him drugs? An arrest then might not be possible.

Fortunately for Stryker, his ghost – an undercover who accompanies the buyer, or in this case, was nearby, as a safety measure – saw the seller, described him down to the color of his sneakers and paved the way for an easy-as-pie arrest.

"I was ready," Stryker said. "Just not as ready as I thought I was. But I did make the buy so I knew I could do it and I knew I'd get better with practice."

###########

And get better he did, making one successful buy after another and contributing to scores of investigations, small ones at first, then those bigger in scale – more drugs, more players, more NYPD bosses watching. Within a year, his reputation had soared and it wasn't uncommon for Stryker to get lent out to other units, other supervisors, even other boroughs.

"It felt real good," Stryker allows. "But I was just glad I was getting the job done, making a difference any way I could."

Often, as with most undercovers, it was done with his guile and his story-telling ability, as in a case regarding drug dealing near Hale House.

Mother Clara Hale by then was a national icon, a humble woman from North Carolina who in 1969 opened an orphanage in her Harlem brownstone, accepting as her own babies from the worst lot in life – abandoned at birth by their drug-addicted mothers, many infected with AIDS or the virus that causes it.

Unfortunately, however, drug dealers thought nothing of selling dope on her block, West 122nd Street in Harlem.

Stryker, working undercover, walked up to a dealer one day looking to score.

"You don't look like someone that smokes," the skeptical dealer said.

"You're right, but if you need to know, my aunt is a teacher at the school right here and cannot be caught buying this from you," Stryker said with a puppy dog look. "So I look out for her because she lets me live with her."

The dealer had likely never heard that one before. He fell for the ruse.

"Good for you looking out for your aunt," he said.

Then he sold Stryker three bags of crack and was arrested.

On another occasion, a skeptical dealer pressed Stryker for information about who he was.

"Where you from?" he wanted to know. "Where you from?"

"A few blocks away. 129th Street."

"What building?"

"Yo, I'm from around here," Stryker shot back. "I live around here all my life. I never seen you before. You a cop?"

He started walking away.

"Maybe this ain't a good idea."

Panicked, the dealer got in front of Stryker.

"Nah, man. It's cool. Whatcha need?"

Sale completed.

Stryker appreciated the skepticism. He realized it was a by-product of what police were doing out there. They wouldn't be so nervous if police were letting them sell wherever and whenever they wanted.

Still, he made sure to play to the hilt the role of the frustrated buyer.

"Where you from?" another dealer asked him. "Who you buying for?"

"I'm buyin,' man. I'm buyin.' No matter for who."

"It's just that I don't recognize you," the dealer said. "Who you with?"

"Yo," Stryker told him, "you're asking me questions like this is some sort of job interview, dude. I understand you're careful, man, but scared money is no money."

Not wanting to lose a customer, the dealer relented, sold to Stryker and was under arrest the minute Stryker walked away and turned the corner.

While Stryker was still relatively new to the undercover game one of his supervisors, a sergeant, used him to teach his more veteran cops a lesson. He had Stryker head to another office in the building where he was assigned and pass himself off as a cadet.

"Today's my dress down day," he explained. "Normally, I have my uniform on but the boss is real good to me. Anyway, I need to get your IDs so I can get copies for the office, for the files."

Then, as they reached for the ID cards, he chatted them up, asking about their experiences, wondering where he should try to work once he joins the force.

He walked out with 30 IDs, no questions asked. Hours later, as their tour ended, the savvy veterans realized the cadet never brought their ID cards back.

They went looking for "that kid."

"What kid?" the sergeant asked. "What…Oh, no. Oh, my God, that sonofabitch managed to get past security again. He did the same thing last week."

The sergeant ran out of there like his pants were on fire, ostensibly to tell his boss what just happened.

He returned a few minutes later.

"Looks can be deceiving," he told them. "That kid is one of us, a new undercover. You guys are experienced undercovers and investigators. You have to remember: you can't think everybody's a bad guy. And you can't think everybody's a good guy."

Stryker's bosses were impressed when they heard how he scammed an entire team of veterans, and his evaluations reflected that. They were convinced they had found themselves a keeper.

CHAPTER 7 – THE PREDICATE CASE

Stryker's first gun buy was routine – he made it from a dealer who was also selling cocaine. But it showed to his supervisors that Stryker could take his game a step up. He could buy drugs. Now, he could also buy guns. And he could do both on the same day, sometimes from different sellers in completely separate cases.

"It's all about making money for these guys, whether they're selling drugs or guns," Stryker explained. "But when you're dealing with guns things are obviously way more dangerous. The guy selling crack on the corner, the little guy, he probably doesn't have a gun. Not so with the guy selling you a gun – he can shoot you with the same gun you went up to him to buy if he thinks you're a cop or if you piss him off somehow."

############

By the time the residents of West 124th Street had started complaining about crack on their block, the drug crew in question, believed by police to be led by a convicted dealer named Collyer Goodman, was a well-oiled machine, pulling in tens of thousands of dollars a week. His stash house was an apartment in a building on that block, and his dealers plied their trade openly, engaged in quick sales in front of the same building – just a half-block away from where kids and families liked to gather in Marcus Garvey Park – or just around the corner on Lenox Avenue, also known as Malcolm X Boulevard.

The kites, police jargon for complaints from the public about a location, were a source of great concern at the 28th Precinct stationhouse.

In response, a midnight narcotics team was dispatched to do something about it. Undercovers went to work trying to make buys and work their way up the ladder. Bust a street seller, persuade him to cooperate, target the mid-level manager, bust him, persuade him to cooperate, and so on, and so on.

Classic police work – except that it didn't work out as planned. The midnight team was spinning its wheels, making street buys, certainly, but it was not having any luck in working its way up the crew's ladder and bringing the hierarchy to its knees. The arrests that were being made, even occurring in the dead of night, should have been enough to appease the public, and to a certain extent, NYPD brass.

But this was early 2000. Crime in New York City was not the overwhelming concern it had once been. Whereas 10 years earlier most New Yorkers would be thankful just to make it home alive – and most precinct commanders considered it a success just to make it through a day without someone getting murdered – by the new millennium expectations had shifted dramatically.

Bratton had returned, this time as police commissioner, when Rudolph Giuliani took over as mayor of New York City in 1994. It was not a marriage made in heaven.

Bratton resigned after 27 months, though in essence he had been pushed out by Giuliani, a man who had an insatiable need for the spotlight and had grown tired – some say envious – of the attention Bratton had been accorded by the media. The breaking point was a *Time Magazine* cover story that lavished praise on Bratton and his quick success in driving crime down.

But while Bratton was done, the CompStat system he instituted was still in place and in fact was being emulated by police departments across the country.

By then, the CompStat legend had been burnished. Jack Maple, a trusted lieutenant in Bratton's inner circle, had sided up to the bar one night in the Oak Room, the clubby watering hole at the Plaza Hotel, across from Central Park. He pulled out a pen and scribbled on a napkin what would be the template for CompStat, short for computer statistics: track and map crimes as they happen, then respond accordingly. It spoke to a philosophy that police can, should and would fight crime in a proactive, rather than reactive, manner, that the crime rate was something that could be driven down. Why no one thought of this sooner is remarkable, given its simplicity.

But bureaucracies tend to work this way: things get done a certain way because they've always been done that certain way. Now shut up, do your job, collect your paycheck and retire after 20 years with a nice pension. Maple thought differently. And Bratton, to his credit, saw the wisdom in Maple's idea.

Their philosophy was basic: If you're running a precinct, you better know everything that's going on there. Someone's stealing Cadillacs all of a sudden? Then what recidivist car thief just got paroled and is back home? Junior high kids are getting mugged outside McDonald's on their way home from school? Why don't you have more officers posted outside that McDonald's? Two masked gunman have struck at bodegas the last eight Saturday nights? Well, in the name of Jesus H. Christ why is your anti-crime team working Monday to Friday, 8 a.m. to 4 p.m.? This is police work, not some insurance office. Make yourself accountable or you're transferred. Get the job done or we'll find someone who can.

The media lapped it up, reporting one story after another about the dramatic drop in crime, as well as the hardball tactics on full display at the weekly CompStat meetings held at One Police Plaza. Commanders – smart, accomplished career cops who knew how to get results – were too often driven to the brink of nervous breakdowns as they prepared to get drilled. In one legendary and embarrassing incident, Pinocchio's long nose flashed on a projector screen to express skepticism about how a particular police supervisor was fighting crime. During other meetings there were threats and even a near fight.

But the pressures, however unfair, did produce results. Murders, which had started dropping during the tenure of Bratton's predecessor, Raymond Kelly, fell even more dramatically under Bratton. There were 1,946 murders in 1993, then 1,561 in 1994, then 1,177 in 1995. By 2000, the number was down to 673. Unimaginable at the height of the bad old days, yet true. Residents across the city rejoiced, and they now had an increased sense of empowerment, knowing full well that precinct commanders were held to a higher level of accountability than ever before. There was, after all, less violent crime to contend with, meaning more time could be spent focusing on other offenses, such as street-level drug dealing.

So when the midnight team failed to bring down the crew making life uncomfortable for residents of West 124th Street the NYPD turned to Plan B.

Enter Stryker and his colleagues.

############

The handoff from one unit to the other is often fraught with mistakes, missteps and miscommunications. In track and field, many a gold medal have been lost as one runner botched the baton pass to the next runner, holding it too high or too low, or maybe dropping it altogether. In the newspaper business, when day editors brief night editors, it is not uncommon for information to get lost in the shuffle. End result: the story in print the next day is missing key information. And in retail, the inability of one manager to inform the next of a shortage of a certain item – cinnamon, for instance, in a bakery – means lost dollars.

In police work, such errors can prove fatal. So how do you avoid them? For one thing, the team taking over a case makes sure to sit down with the team handing off the case to learn as much as possible about all the players.

Detective Mike Paul was the case officer assigned to learn anything and everything about Collyer Goodman and his crew, then fully prep Stryker and the rest of the team.

His philosophy? Know your enemy.

"If you're gonna send me somewhere I need to know who we think is the killer, who we think is a punk, who we think is a snitch, so that way when I'm sitting down at the table I know who I'm dealing with and how I should play things," Paul said. "Plus, you gotta get the rap sheets on everybody. This guy was collared for petty larceny, shoplifting. This other one was collared for armed robbery. So if anything goes bad, he's probably the first one who's gonna make a move. I'm not saying the shoplifting guy won't do it neither, but it's good to know which guy has already been violent."

Goodman was a tough guy, didn't talk much to anyone. Very arrogant, with a swagger about him, Paul remembered. Oh, and of course, he was difficult to get to, which is why Paul was involved in the case to begin with.

The best drug dealers are the ones police don't know much about.

They operate carefully, layers and layers of underlings separating them from the guy buying on the street. They delegate. If they talk on the phone, it's only briefly, and never for any length of time on the same phone. They use burners, cheap, prepaid phones bought with cash and dumped after a week or so of use in favor of another burner. The smart dealers try not to bring attention to themselves with flashy cars, flashier jewelry and even gaudier homes. For law enforcement, identifying these dealers takes time and arresting them takes even longer.

Collyer Goodman might have known that at some point, but eventually his hubris would do him in.

He had lived a seemingly charmed life until then. Born December 8th, 1974, Collyer Goodman grew into a 5-foot-11 inch, 220-pound repeat offender. He kicked off his criminal career at age 15 when he was busted and accused of selling drugs seven days before Christmas. As with most first-time offenders, the system went relatively easy on him. The sale charges were dismissed and Goodman was sentenced as a juvenile to reform school.

In 1992, just past his 17th birthday, Goodman was at it again, caught with drugs and, after pleading guilty, sentenced to five years' probation. Of course, he did not behave himself, charged just three months before his 18th birthday with raping and sodomizing his girlfriend. With the arrest came a search warrant of his apartment on West 124th Street. Inside, police found 158 vials of crack, a scale and over $2,100 in cash. Goodman didn't lie about it, either, telling the court he was a drug dealer. He pleaded guilty to drug charges and on March 25th, 1993, Goodman, now an adult, was again sentenced to probation.

If Goodman learned anything, rehabilitation wasn't it. Four months into his probation, Goodman was again renewing acquaintances with the NYPD. On July 1st, 1993, police raided the same Harlem apartment and caught him trying to throw away a box holding cocaine and a loaded 9mm handgun. Thirteen days later, he was accused of selling crack to an undercover in the lobby of a building. He wasn't a kingpin and the evidence didn't suggest he was a major player – at least not yet. Still, he was put behind bars, sentenced to two to four years in prison after pleading guilty in both cases.

After he got out he remained on parole until July 1997 and behaved himself, at least as far as authorities could document, until September of that year, when he was arrested for drug and weapons possession and sentenced to a few months in jail. He got out again and, you guessed it, got arrested again, this time during a buy and bust drop operation on his block. He also had a switchblade on him and pleaded to fourth-degree weapons possession, a misdemeanor. None of his cases – 15 total, 13 of which were felonies – stood out in any particular way. They didn't make the papers. Only one involved a gun. Goodman didn't kill anyone, fire at a cop or mug an old lady.

Social media hadn't yet been introduced, so aside from the usual posturing that came being King Shit – or at least thinking he was King Shit – Goodman was known to few beyond his family, his posse and the NYPD. He was known by his real name, of course, but also a host of other names – Collyer R. Goodman, Collior Goodman, Couyer Goodman, Colley Goodman, Carl Goodman, Collyer West, Carl West and Derrick R. Hollis.

All were provided in an attempt to confuse authorities and increase the chance his next bust appeared to be his first and might make some rookie cop or prosecutor go easy on him. The law knew better, though its efforts did little to curtail Goodman's criminal ways. He was, in fact, at one point a target in a federal Bronx drug probe. Others were busted, but Goodman avoided arrest.

And so, perhaps emboldened by a growing sense that long prison sentences were for the sloppy, the foolhardy and those who couldn't afford a high-priced lawyer, Goodman allowed his vanity to get the best of him, tooling around town in a tan Cadillac Escalade that was shiny enough to look gold and that practically screamed DRUG DEALER!

Specially equipped with two video monitors and an underside lighting system, the Escalade lit up wherever it went. And when it was parked, it was bathed in light and looked even better than it really was.

"It looked like the car was in a spotlight," Stryker said. "Yeah, he thought he was 'The Man.' But you know what? The guy who's 'The Man' doesn't have to say he's 'The Man.' The guy who thinks he's 'The Man' really isn't. He thought that he was. It was my job to show him he wasn't."

Working with Stryker and his colleagues was the Office of the Special Narcotics Prosecutor, headed by Bridget Brennan. An independent agency with citywide jurisdiction, the agency was created in 1971 in response to the booming heroin epidemic and the violent crime that accompanied it. When heroin use waned – its popularity rises and falls, depending on myriad factors – the office remained in place, often serving as the agency police would turn to when it desperately needed a victory in court.

The five district attorneys' offices that serve New York City are saturated with top-notch prosecutors, but each has its own daily burdens that often get in the way of the big picture. Special Narcotics was far less complicated. It could focus on far fewer cases than any district attorney's office, with a particular emphasis on taking down entire crews and their leaders.

To nail Goodman, though, Stryker had to deal with the little fish, the underlings whose sole importance would be to serve as a stepping stone to reaching Goodman.

"I knew we could get this guy," Stryker remembered. "We just had to put the time in, but I was confident – we all were confident – that we could get it done."

Indeed, just three months earlier, Stryker, with some 500 drug purchases under his belt, had scored high on his performance evaluation for the previous year.

"Detective Stryker evaluates information as it develops and adjusts his techniques in approaching his targeted subjects," a supervisor wrote. "He reacts calmly as conditions change and develops strategy for the team prior to any enforcement action. The detective communicates with targeted subjects in a street demeanor which not all undercover officers can master. He successfully operates in all types of neighborhoods."

Impressive.

But Goodman was a new target. Would Stryker slip up? Would Goodman be more than his equal? Would the case succeed or fail? Paul had done all he could. Now it was Stryker's turn.

Naturally, the first buy was not with Goodman but rather with one of the little fish in his pond.

At about 11 p.m. on September 28th, 2000, Stryker and Detective Leroy Dressler slipped into the lobby of 64 West 124th Street and met with Craz, a young turk in Goodman's crew, and Bad Boy, later determined to be Rory Johnson. An informant of Paul's had smoothed the way so this deal could go down. Still, there was wariness all around. Like the car dealer who has to run the sale by his boss, Johnson said there was no way he'd sell anything to someone he'd never met unless the big man signed off on it. He called Goodman, nickname Wes – though at the time for all Stryker knew Johnson could have been talking to his grandmother – and briefed him.

Deal – 40 glassines of crack for $200.

The drugs and the cash, pre-recorded, with its serial numbers written down, were the first pieces of evidence in the case.

And by the way, Johnson told Stryker, "I work for Wes."

Now, it was like dating. Should Stryker call the next day? Should he wait for him to call? Stryker didn't want to seem desperate. But what if he waited too long? Johnson might meet someone else.

The Goodman crew knew Stryker's storyline, that is, the dealers knew what Stryker had told them. He ran out of Coney Island and needed a reliable supplier. Nothing too big. He was down on the rung and answered to his own bosses. If the bosses liked the product and if the customers came back for more, well, then, he'd come back to Harlem for more.

Two weeks later – a little long for a second date, but hey, they were still talking – Stryker was, as promised, back for more. Same location, but now the meet was for 7 p.m. Hmmm. Why the change of time? Cause for concern? Maybe. Maybe not. This time, the seller was a guy named Kilo – not his real name, of course. He was with Wes, he let it be known.

I'm with the NYPD, you stupid ass, Stryker thought to himself.

The deal was a walk in the park – another 40 bags of crack for $200. Oh, and would you have any guns you'd be interested in selling? Two small drug buys into the courtship and Stryker was taking a calculated risk by talking firearms with a crew he was only just beginning to know.

"We got lucky because he had gotten rid of a couple of guys for stealing from him," Stryker said. "So now he was more hands-on than he had been. Plus, I knew how to draw someone like him out. The guy I'm dealing with, he's limited. He's selling me $200 worth of crack. Now, I want $400 worth, so he's gotta go to the boss and the boss is like, 'Who is this guy?' He's thinking to himself, 'I can't trust my guy to sell that much because I've already caught guys stealing from me.' And then when I start talking about buying guns I'm thinking that he's gotta be paying attention, wondering who I am. So what does he do? Now, he's gotta come see me for himself. Now, I'm buying from him, the boss."

Kilo agreed to talk to Goodman about guns. But as expected it didn't happen overnight.

A month later, Stryker bought coke from Johnson – $440 worth. Two weeks after that, another coke buy, with a gun deal finally agreed upon for the next day, December 1st. It went down without a hitch – Stryker handing Johnson $400 on the corner of West 112th Street and Mount Morris Park West, 7:30 p.m., late enough to be dark outside. Stryker walked away with a Smith & Wesson .38-caliber revolver.

If Goodman was intrigued by this new buyer he wasn't yet showing it. At least not in person. There were no more buys for a while – again, not unusual, as undercovers never want to come off as too eager because they don't want to get made as cops. On top of that, Goodman's crew seemed concerned about a police presence they noticed in the building, or at least thought they noticed. But any such presence was coincidental. The precinct was aware of the undercover probe going on and had made a point of not going to the West 124th Street building unless someone called 911.

In the end, it was a minor worry, and when the next sale went down on April 3rd, 2001, it took place across the street with Johnson and a guy known as "Gotti" – how thoroughly unoriginal! – selling Stryker five dime bags. The next day two new players were introduced into the mix, a guy named Lite and Goodman himself. Lite said he worked for Goodman.

That's right, Goodman concurred, all but declaring himself the boss. Lite sold Stryker 13 grams of coke for $480. More importantly, he gave Stryker Goodman's number and promised to do better the next time on the price he charged.

Bingo!

A week later – again, the idea was not to come across as too eager – Stryker dialed Goodman's number. They agreed to meet, with Stryker buying 12 grams of coke for $400, a cheaper price, per gram, as Goodman promised. Two weeks later, it was 65 grams for $2,200.

Now it was clear Goodman trusted Stryker.

Paul was not surprised.

"Stevie's got a way about him," Paul said. "You instantly like him."

Stryker, meanwhile, sensed he had hooked Goodman. So he tried reeling him in.

"I mentioned guns to him. 'Yo, I got some beef in Coney Island with some Crips.' I knew he'd listen because up where Goodman is everyone's Bloods. So he's like, 'We'll come to Brooklyn and help you out.' But I talked him down. I told him I didn't want him to ruin his business for me and that I'd handle it if he could get his hands on some firepower."

On May 3rd, 2001, Goodman and two underlings, Irvin Fields, aka Uncle Pete, and Jihad Allen, aka CEO, met with Stryker and Dressler to talk about selling and buying guns.

Goodman by now had been bragging about what drug dealing had afforded him. The Escalade. The bail for the inevitable arrests of his young bucks. The expensive private attorney, the kind with custom-made suits, not the Legal Aid types with their off-the-rack sport jackets.

He talked about being untouchable. He talked about having cops in his family. He talked about getting away with whatever he wanted to get away with. Blah, blah, blah.

He had even offered to take Stryker to Atlantic City to watch a boxing match.

Stryker, a fight fan, relished the idea but thought better of it.

"I told him my crew worked for the Colombians and I had to go see them that weekend," Stryker remembered.

Another time, Goodman, all set to sell Stryker cocaine and a gun, noticed that his new best friend looked like shit.

"I used to suffer from allergies real bad," Stryker said. "One time I show up, my eyes are bloodshot red. My nose was stuffy, constantly sneezing. Wes goes, 'You all right? What's wrong with you?'

"I'm like, 'It's just my allergies.'"

"Yo, go to my man around the corner. He's got the Jamaican store."

Stryker would've eaten garbage at that point if it would have him feel better. So off he went. Dressler was with him that day, and he was leery, to say the least. He warned Stryker this Jamaican magic man might be feeding him an illegal drug. And with his luck the department would call him in the next day for a random drug test.

"I go over there and I tell the guy, 'Yo, I heard you got something good for the allergies. My man Wes sent me.' He gave me this little red pill and I swear to you in 10 minutes my allergies were gone. Like they never even happened."

But Stryker was soon in la-la land, suspended somewhere between reality and an alternate universe.

"You better hope you don't get tested tomorrow," Dressler told him.

"Nah, it's like Sudafed."

Goodman was thrilled to see Stryker was feeling better. He also revealed another piece of himself that day. He declared himself a rapper. Just like every other guy out on the streets, Stryker thought to himself. He'd be a millionaire 10 times over if even one-tenth of the dealers who claimed they were rappers or rap producers actually were rappers or rap producers.

But Goodman also said he had a self-financed record label, Predicate Records, and that he had got a couple of local rappers who had put together enough songs for a compact disc. Financed from his drug money, Stryker assumed.

"We were standing on the corner, right by his Cadillac, and he's like, 'Check this out.' Pops in the CD. Boom, boom, ah, boom. Just like we were in the club. I looked at the CD. It looked professional. The cover art said Predicate Records in black with a white background."

Goodman even incorporated the label – Predicate Enterprises, Inc.

Stryker bought a CD on the spot for $10, a transaction that would later be memorialized in court as Exhibit A. He sold 10 copies of the CD in Coney Island – at least that is what he told Goodman – and returned to him $100. Goodman was thrilled.

Stryker by then was telling his supervisors that he had Goodman hooked and that he'd likely be able to go even higher up the food chain and at the very least figure out who was supplying Goodman.

He probably didn't have to travel far, three miles north into Washington Heights, to find Goodman's dealer. From there, who knew where the trail would take investigators. Colombia? Mexico? He figured the Drug Enforcement Administration would likely be called in and what started with a few complaints from pissed-off residents would turn into an international case prosecuted in federal court.

But no major drug prosecution is ever easy. A slam dunk case fizzles. An untouchable target suddenly seems in reach – and then he's not. A promising lead turns into a dead end.

In this case, the end came unexpectedly and abruptly. In a free-wheeling conversation with his new best friend, Goodman talked openly about future drug sales, installing traps in their cars to hide contraband, and, oh, yeah, monitoring police radios.

"You want a police radio?" Goodman asked.

At first, Stryker sloughed Goodman off. Yes, Goodman had bragged about police in the family and being untouchable.

But that's a common trick among dealers looking to convince new buyers there's no need to worry about the police. He could get a scanner anywhere, such as the nearby Radio Shack. Not those radios, Goodman said. Actual NYPD radios. The ones cops use.

Stryker's ears perked up. Having a police radio can give any bad guy, not to mention a savvy player like Goodman, a distinct, possibly a deadly, advantage. You know where the cops are coming from? Lie in wait and take one out. You want a hit on a rival to go down smoothly? Press the button, call in a 10-13 – "Officer down! Officer down!" – a dozen blocks away, then watch as police cars race past, giving you ample opportunity to commit murder and avoid getting caught.

"You can pick up all the lingo, the way us cops speak, use it your advantage," Stryker said. "A patrol radio is like a pearl in a bad guy's hand."

Still, the cynic in Stryker figured Goodman was full of shit.

"Whatever."

And for a while, it was just that – whatever. Goodman gave Stryker his number, sold him more crack and told him he had another 10 kilos of coke in his home. Then, a few weeks later, Goodman proved to be a man of his word.

"I got that for you," Goodman told Stryker and Dressler.

"Got what?" Stryker asked?

"A radio."

"Yo, I told you I'm not buying no scanner."

"Wait here."

Goodman walked away, and Stryker and Dressler didn't know what to think.

"All of sudden," Stryker remembered, "you hear 'Sector Adam to central' and I'm like, 'Are there cops in the building?'"

There came Goodman with a bonafide NYPD radio. That day, Stryker bought from Goodman coke, a .40-caliber handgun and the radio. He gave Goodman $3,400 in cash, each bill's serial number carefully documented and placed in the growing file being used to build a case against him.

Back at the office his team looked at the radio as if they were staring at an alien from outer space.

"How the fuck did Goodman get his hands on that?" one supervisor asked.

The team at that point had two options: Ignore the radio and keep working Goodman until Stryker reached his supplier or follow protocol and notify the Internal Affairs Bureau about the radio. As part of its many duties, IAB investigates any incident involving lost or stolen NYPD property. Did some cop get sloppy and leave his gun or radio in an unmarked car? Has he done this before? Or was he a rogue cop selling his wares? Such an investigation typically trumped all others, including the Goodman narcotics probe.

"Believe me we thought about leaving IAB out of this, but our sergeant said there was no way we could do that," Stryker said.

IAB was called. Within a few days the order came down: the Goodman probe was over.

Goodman was arrested soon after. He was no longer so brazen.

Staring at life in prison, he implicated Police Officer Derwin Blanks, identifying him as a distant cousin and claiming Blanks had given him the police radio and was a part of his operation, authorities said at the time.

Internal Affairs investigators set up a sting, arresting Blanks when he picked up half a kilo of cocaine – worth $15,000 to $20,000 – and drove to a street in Washington Heights, leaving the drugs in the car, ostensibly for Goodman's partners. Instead, Internal Affairs stepped forward and slapped the handcuffs on him. Blanks ultimately pleaded guilty to drug possession charges.

Goodman, meanwhile, pleaded to drug and gun charges and faced seven years to life in prison. He applied for re-sentencing under the Drug Law Reform Act but was denied in 2006. He was released from prison in 2011.

Two of his minions, Johnson and Price, pleaded to drug charges and served a few years in prison.

Not the home run everyone hoped for.

Still, on the day police moved in, confiscated Goodman's Escalade and searched his apartment on West 124th Street, it was clear who the real winners were.

As Goodman was being handcuffed neighbors began clapping. Other police officers, meanwhile, were carting out evidence of Goodman's operation, including five guns, one of them a machine gun.

That acknowledgment from residents, Stryker said, made his work worth it.

############

Harlem today looks nothing like the Harlem of 1990. Crumbling shells of once grand brownstones could be had for $1 back then. Today, they're fully renovated and will set you back more than $1 million, easily.

Fast food restaurants, cheap liquor stores and check cashing shops dotted the landscape back then – not just Harlem but also Washington Heights, then the cocaine capital of America. Today, Starbucks has moved in, as have celebrity chefs, fancy clothing boutiques and a wave of new money. President Bill Clinton, after leaving office, set up an office in Harlem.

To be sure, Harlem is less black than it once was – and whites are also growing in numbers in Washington Heights and in Inwood, the smaller neighborhood at the northern tip of Manhattan. Amid soaring real estate prices is the debate over gentrification and the changes it brings.

Still, there can be no arguing with the miraculous drop in crime, the sharp drop in open-air drug selling and the near disappearance of the pervasive fear that something bad could happen at any time.

"We did that," Stryker said. "We started that. Is it bragging? Sure is. But you couldn't walk the streets up there without fearing for your life.

"We got rid of that."

Several months after Goodman was convicted, however, Stryker, and the rest of the NYPD for that matter, got a stern reminder about just how frightening undercover work could be.

Stryker's fifth child, Timothy,* had been born and the family was all smiles as everyone headed home from the hospital.

Nothing looked amiss, at least at first. But then Stryker's wife went upstairs and found, in the dresser drawer of the bedroom where their 10-year-old son slept, a hole that was not part of any furniture design. There, atop a stack of T-shirts, was a .45-caliber bullet.

Stryker's eyes widened.

Undercovers go to great lengths to conceal their identity. They choose street names and back stories that they can easily remember and they don't reveal their true selves. They regularly change the routes they take to and from work. They try as best they can not to eat or socialize in areas where they've made buys. And the NYPD also helps by limiting the number of people who know an undercover's real name.

Some undercovers, particularly those who work in the Intelligence Bureau on terrorism investigations, get plucked from the Police Academy. Before they're ever introduced to a precinct commander or paired up with a uniformed partner, they're gone. The other recruits are told nothing and just assume a past misdeed finally caught up with their missing academy mate.

For undercovers like Stryker, the task is a little greater. They've been out there, on the street, in uniform, in different neighborhoods. They've been supervised, paired with different partners, made arrests and testified in open court before going undercover. In short, a whole lot more people know who they are, even as the NYPD strikes their names from the numerous department databases and assigns them an undercover number. Even in court, that's how they are identified.

How did this happen? What, Stryker asked himself, had he done wrong? Where did he slip up? As all this raced through his mind, Stryker ran back downstairs and out to the front of his house. There it was – an unmistakable bullet hole next to his son's window. Next to that hole was a second, a 9mm bullet stuck inside, not quite powerful enough to penetrate the wall, though clearly the gunman or gunmen had been aiming, if not for the window, then certainly for the house.

Neighbors on Stryker's block had always wondered about him. His close friends knew he was a cop, though they just assumed he worked patrol. Others weren't so sure what he did.

"I was always driving different cars, dressing flashy, coming home at all hours," Stryker said. "No doubt some people thought I was a drug dealer, or a rapper."

The police response to his 911 call, however, cleared up whatever questions his neighbors had. By day's end, there was a patrol car stationed in front of his house, and, given that it was a two-way street, a second one was posted on the corner and a third one on the opposite corner. For good measure, the NYPD installed a panic button in the home to put Charlene at ease.

Suspicion fell on Goodman and Blanks and others Stryker had helped put behind bars, including those sprung from behind bars in recent months. The culprit, however, was never found. The sound of gunfire at a nearby housing project was not uncommon, but Stryker didn't work in the area where he lived so any connection there seemed unlikely. In the end, the gunman may have been some punk who just decided to let off a few rounds as he drove by and wound up striking a cop's house.

Still, Charlene wanted out of the house. Pack your bags, we are gone.

"We're living in the safest house in America, right now – other than the White House," Stryker told her. "We'll be fine."

The police presence proved an inconvenience for everyone on the block, but for three months the otherwise safe block was indeed much safer.

The Strykers decided to stay right there.

CHAPTER 8 – HUMOR

Nothing like a hilarious, you-can't-make-this-shit-up moment to cut the tension while working undercover.

Stryker loved nothing more than taking guns off the street. One by one. In groups. From young men. From veteran criminals. Didn't matter if they were old guns with a history of bloodshed on them or new ones just sold down south, where it's much easier to buy a weapon, then transported along the Iron Pipeline, the stretch of Interstate 95 that runs up to New York City. A gun on the street meant there was always work to do.

In Manny, a gun dealer, Stryker had himself an all too eager seller. One evening, in the shadow of the elevated subway that sends the No. 1 train roaring into the Bronx, just past the tip of northern Manhattan, Stryker and another undercover sat in their car. Manny slipped in, sold them two guns, then got greedy and stupid.

"Yo, listen, I got another gun upstairs."

Sure. Why not? Go get it.

Most buys never go exactly according to plan. You go for one gun, you come back with three. You go for three, you come back with none.

No different than most shopping excursions. Except, of course, that you can get killed buying guns. Still, Stryker wanted to take as many off the streets as possible.

"What kinda gun?" he asked Manny.

"It's like a rifle," Manny said, dead serious.

Stryker and his partner could have burst out laughing right there. A rifle? In New York City? Certainly there are those who live in New York City, own rifles and go upstate every fall to hunt deer and other game.

But the detectives, playing homeboys out of Brooklyn, were not two such people.

"Now, we're not gonna tell him that." Stryker remembered. "We're not gonna tell him to get lost. I'm like, 'Dude, I'm not going hunting elephant. What the hell am I gonna do with a rifle?'

"But I want the gun. I'll take any gun. A rifle is just a misdemeanor. I'm after the felony, so I played like I didn't want it, but at the end I knew I was gonna buy it."

Not yet sure if he had a sale, Manny persisted until he reached a deal.

"Go get the gun," Stryker told him.

If Manny never returned, no one would have been surprised.

But he came back with a big bag that looked like it was holding, well, a rifle.

He got in the car and showed the detectives the weapon.

"Do I look like I'm going to Africa to shoot something?" Stryker wanted to know.

Manny persisted.

"Give me a price. Whatcha wanna give me?"

Stryker played hard to get.

"Nah, man, I can't be out here with something that big. I can't stand out in the middle of Coney Island with this. Now, if it was a sawed-off rifle, maybe. I gotta be able to stick it in my coat."

Manny was intrigued.

"You got a saw?" Stryker wondered. "If you got a saw and can cut it down, then we'll see."

Stryker's already had this guy on the hook for two guns. A third would make the case stronger. Better yet, sawing the barrel down to less than 18 inches would turn possession of the rifle into a felony.

"I'll get a saw," Manny said.

He popped out of the car. When he came back about a half-hour later he was exhausted, dripping sweat and practically panting. But he had the rifle, sawed-off barrel and all.

Still, it wasn't short enough.

"Gotta be shorter than that."

He left to go back to his apartment. This guy was apparently really determined to get rid of his rifle.

By then, Stryker and his partner were pissing their pants with laughter. Their sergeant, listening in on the kel, was not so amused. Was this even legal? Are we entrapping him? Another half hour went by before Manny returned.

But this time he had someone with him, some guy carrying the saw.

"Is this for real?" Saw Man wanted to know.

"Yo," Stryker shot back. "You cut that down short enough you got yourself a deal."

And so they went, Manny and Saw Man, back upstairs.

A short time later they returned, but again the gun was too long. Back upstairs Manny and Saw Man went.

When Manny returned yet again he was alone. This time, the rifle was short enough.

Stryker looked at it. Racked it. Gave it the seal of approval.

"Now, we're good to go."

############

Stryker's father always taught him to get back up when he failed. He probably wasn't talking about buying cocaine when he said it. Still, the lesson was learned.

"Let me get three glassine envelopes," Stryker told the dealer. "Let me get three."

In a bodega, the guy behind the counter doesn't give a shit if he knows you. But this wasn't a bodega.

"Who the fuck are you?" came the reply. "I don't know you."

But Stryker wanted to know him.

"Yo, I'm watching you dealing to other people. Why not me?"

"Step off, shorty."

At that point, Stryker could have shrugged and went somewhere else. Or maybe sent another undercover over there. The third option, the one that cops considered settling, would be to retreat, watch from the distance as the dealer sold to someone else, a real drug user, then snatch him up. That's known as an observation arrest.

It was still a felony, Sergeant Vic Sanchez told Stryker, not a meaningless misdemeanor.

"But I want a hand-to-hand," Stryker said, cop parlance for a buy made directly from a dealer.

A hand-to-hand goes down cleaner in court. The cop's word versus the dealer's. The dealer can deny it all he wants. But if the conversation is captured on the wire it's difficult to argue entrapment.

"So I wait like 10 minutes, then I go back to the same guy. He's like, 'Yeah?' and I'm like, 'Yo, we met like 10 minutes ago. We know each other now, even though you didn't give me a chance to introduce myself.'"

The dealer half chuckled.

"Whatcha need, shorty?"

Sanchez, sitting in a van and listening on the kel, laughed approvingly.

"I'm just trying to get three for my daddy," Stryker said.

Deal.

Stryker walked off.

A few minutes later, the dealer didn't know what hit him, cop cars coming at him from three different directions.

Stryker by then was long gone, onto the next buy.

He used a similar tact later in his career when Izzy, a new female undercover, apprenticed under him to learn the ropes.

Her first week as an undercover she walked up on two guys dealing on West 123rd Street in Harlem.

She wanted two vials of crack, green top, as in the green vial caps. But the dealers looked at her like she was from another planet.

"They're asking her who she is, where's she from, how they never seen her before, then they try to get her to go with them into a building," Stryker remembered. "I had told her again and again not to ever go inside with guys you're trying to buy from."

She heeded the advice, refusing to enter the building.

They were not happy.

"Get outta here, bitch."

Stryker was watching this from several hundred feet away.

"Negative buy," she mumbled. "They won't sell to me."

No sweat, the sergeant said. Move to next spot and have her try there. Stryker admittedly didn't like working with women undercovers. He was old school and felt he had to be overly protective of them even though he knew some could probably kick his ass. Whatever the reason, he wanted Izzy to feel better about herself.

"No, sarge. Let me give it a crack."

These two guys had never seen Stryker before either, but he saw a way in as he sauntered over to them.

"What's up, brothers?" he asked.

"What's up, shorty?"

"Yeah, that bitch just asked me to sell to her," Stryker said. "But I was a little suspect, know what I'm sayin'?"

They agreed.

"Sure do," one of them said. "I been here longer than a moment and I ain't never seen her."

"Yo," Stryker told them. "Let me get three. Green tops."

How these dealers weren't now suspicious of Stryker was anyone's guess.

After all, he had just told them that Izzy had tried to buy from him. Sure, it was possible he had just run out of his stash of crack. But why would he come to them? Wouldn't he go back to his supplier?

"That's the thing," Stryker said. "I got them thinking about the lady detective. And when I said, 'Let me get green tops,' they didn't think anything of it. Matter of fact, how we got the second guy was that the main guy only had two left and he tells his boy, 'Yo, go get some more green.'"

Now, a simple hand-to-hand had implicated both dealers. They were both in cuffs before they could blink.

"And that female undercover became a very, very good undercover. We could have moved to another spot. But I like the challenge. I take it personally. No way I'm gonna let someone stand on this corner and sell and not get caught.

"I won't allow it."

############

Stryker's uncle beat the balls off him one day. Actually, he never laid a hand on him. But the steerer for a drug crew on West 119th Street certainly believed that when Stryker told him.

And he knew the money he made directly depended on this sad sack – Stryker – who walked up to him looking like a scared puppy.

"Anybody working?" Stryker asked.

"Yeah, right here," the steerer said, pointing a short distance away to a small hole in the wall under the staircase of an abandoned building.

The crew had busted in through the roof and set up shop, slinging drugs through a hole barely big enough through which to slip a vial of crack or glassine envelope of cocaine.

"All you can see is the eyeball," Stryker said. "So the field team couldn't get nobody. Who you gonna get? The steerer on the street? Big deal. He just tells you to go to the hole. It's just a waste of time. I'm aware of this and my sergeant tells me we gotta figure out another way. So as I'm approaching all I can hear is him saying 'Stevie, do not buy out of the hole.'"

And Stryker wouldn't, much to the steerer's chagrin.

He tried to get Stryker to change his mind.

"Nah, man, I can't," Stryker explained. "The last time I bought out of the hole and took it to my uncle that dude bugged out. Didn't like the shit and kicked everybody's ass in the house. I got beat up bad and I couldn't tell him who sold it to me. Nah. Never mind – I'll go round the corner to 120th Street."

Now the steerer was picturing his own ass getting kicked, losing business to some rival a block away.

"Give me money, yo – just give me the money."

Stryker saw an opening.

"Yo, what's your name in case my uncle wants to beat me up again?"

"My name's Jake."

That helped, but what about the eyeball? Stryker watched as Jake went to the hole in the wall.

"Yo, Earl, give me three good ones."

Yes!

"So now I got a name. I can't see him, but I got a name. I say, 'Yo, Jake, good looking out, but if it's bad I gotta be able to tell him who Earl is.'"

"My man Earl got a scar on his face, yo," the steerer answered.

Stryker took the drugs and slipped away, never to be seen by Jake again.

About 90 minutes later, Earl left the building and headed to the corner. Stryker's field team pulled up.

Earl's scar was evident.

"Yo, I'm looking for Earl," someone in the car said.

"Yeah, I'm Earl."

"Up against the wall. You're under arrest."

############

The prosecutor, Anne Schwartz, looked at the paperwork for the drug case.

"You gotta be kidding me," she said. "The guy's name is James Bond?"

"That's his name."

Newspapermen kill for anecdotes like this. They can spin entire stories out of the most insignificant of crimes if there's a catchy name involved.

The NYPD once had a chief named Thomas Lawless. In 2014, a man named Messiah was busted in Brooklyn for gun possession – on the day before Easter. And back in 1999, a Brooklyn burglar accidentally hung himself at the Dum Dum Boutique when his sweater got caught on window security bars he tried to slip past.

When Bond's case went to the grand jury Schwartz knew what was coming.

"Detective," she asked Stryker, "What was the defendant's name?"

Straight-faced, or as straight-faced as he could manage, Stryker answered: "Bond. James Bond."

The grand jurors, long-faced and wondering when the hell the day would end, burst out laughing.

############

For another grand jury, Stryker suddenly found himself in the type of situation most undercovers fear: face to face with a dealer from whom he once bought drugs.

But this was in the courthouse, an elevator to be exact.

The dealer was in cuffs, escorted by two other undercovers.

"He sees me as I step on the elevator. He looks at me and I'm thinking, 'I know him,' but I can't quite figure it out. He's like, 'What's up, man?'

and I say the same thing back. I still couldn't quite picture what case I knew him from. But if I bought from him and he got arrested after that, after I left the scene, then he probably put two and two together and figured out I was a cop. Meanwhile, these two cops on the elevator are looking at me and they have no idea who I am."

Stryker, dressed like a drug dealer, could have introduced himself to his brothers in blue. But if he did that, he'd be revealing his identity to the prisoner in handcuffs.

Stryker figured the guy was about to testify. He was right.

"Yeah, last week I testified in the grand jury," Stryker said. "That's good, that's good. Helps your case. Maybe you'll beat the rap."

Sol Wachtler, the former chief judge of New York State, once famously said, "You can indict a ham sandwich," meaning, of course, that if the district attorney really wants to get you indicted, or really doesn't want to get you indicted, then the presentation to the grand jury will reflect that desire.

And so, testifying on your behalf often plays such a small role. That's one school of thought. The other is to get up and say your piece, humanize yourself. Stryker doesn't necessarily believe that – "A lot of these guys are just stupid and testifying would only hurt their cause" – but, hey, it was nine in the morning and that's what he was able to come up with.

"Ya think so?" the prisoner wanted to know.

"Yeah, helped me," Stryker said. "Ya gotta do it."

"Yeah, yeah, I hear ya. Thanks man."

The two cops wanted to slap the handcuffs on Stryker. But later in the day he bumped into them in the hallway and explained himself.

"They were cool and laughing about, but they said they were real pissed when it was happening. We had a good laugh, but stuff like that happens. You never know when you're gonna bump into somebody who knows you or thinks they know you."

CHAPTER 9 – MURDER, THEY WROTE

The Frederick Douglass Houses, home to some 4,500 residents, lie just north of the Upper West Side of Manhattan. Its 17 buildings dominate West 100th Street to West 104th Street, between Amsterdam Avenue and Manhattan Avenue – prime real estate.

It's a housing project – though the New York City Housing Authority, which runs it and more than 300 other projects, considers the term a tabloid pejorative and much more prefers "development."

Whatever the wording, to live in a housing project in modern-day New York City is, for the most part, to live below standard. Too many such projects are in need of an upgrade – basic work in some, dire repairs in others – and far too many are riddled with crime, or are at least more dangerous than life in conventional residential buildings in the same neighborhoods. It is, too often, a tale of two cities.

"Without a struggle, there can be no progress," Frederick Douglass, the abolitionist for whom the houses are named, once said.

Indeed, ridding the Frederick Douglass Houses of drug dealers has proven to be a mighty struggle.

In August 2001, Raynold Mojica was beefing with Darryl Kingsberry, described by authorities at the time as a Bronx drug dealer better known by his street name, Gorilla. At some point, Gorilla, whose uncle lived in a 12th-floor apartment at 875 Amsterdam Avenue, a building in the Frederick Douglass Houses, thought it would be a good idea to move his people in and start selling drugs.

Mojica, employed by Tony Council and Albert Javier, the leaders of a drug crew, told Kingsberry he needed to find another piece of turf.

"Fuck off," Kingsberry told Mojica. He was either unaware who Mojica worked for or he simply didn't give a shit.

Not too smart.

Mojica ran to a "co-worker," EZ, born Ramon Pequero, to fill him on the tensions.

EZ is Javier's cousin. The mother of Javier's children is Council's cousin. All in the family.

EZ, who solved problems the best way he knew how – with violence – made a beeline for Gorilla's uncle's apartment. With him were Mojica and a third associate.

The trio came face-to-face with, among others, Tyrell Williams, age 19. Williams pulled a gun – loaded but inoperable, and kept it at his side. EZ pulled his gun, a .40-caliber revolver, loaded and operable, and shot Williams point blank, once in the chest and once in the forehead.

As Williams fell to the ground dying, his .25-caliber handgun by his side, EZ ran out of the building, hopped into a cab on Amsterdam Avenue and eventually made his way to upstate Albany, some 180 miles away.

Two days after the shooting another Council/Javier underling, Ephrain Gonzalez, had some sharp words with another group of dealers, this one setting up shop at Amsterdam Avenue and West 104th Street. During the argument, a rival dealer named Andre "Dre" Young flashed Gonzalez his gun. Gonzalez, outmanned, left the scene and went right to Council. When Council returned with Gonzalez he decided against gunfire and instead punched one of the dealers, Howie Stokes, right in the face.

Later that night, after the dust had cleared, EZ returned to the same street corner and put a bullet into the back of Al Cruz, who worked with Young and Stokes. Cruz went down in a New York second and EZ stood over him and fired twice more from the same gun used to kill Williams. Somehow, both bullets missed, leaving behind ricochet marks on the sidewalk.

No matter.

Cruz died anyway.

EZ?

He fled to Brooklyn, hiding out in the Marcy Houses, another rough and tumble housing project that had gained cachet as the childhood home of one Shawn Carter, better known as Jay Z. Eventually, EZ, Javier and Council fled to Virginia until the heat died down.

The NYPD and the Manhattan DA's office learned quickly that despite all the witnesses there were none willing to come forward. Everyone saw everything, yet no one saw anything. The "don't snitch" dynamic was on full display. If authorities were going to build a case it was not going to be easy.

Then came September 11th, 2001.

The terror attack at the World Trade Center was met with an unprecedented police response. Cops of all ranks rushed to lower Manhattan from precincts all over the city, from their homes in the five boroughs and beyond and even from out-of-state vacations. If there ever was a time for everyday criminals to have a field day – stick-up men, thieves and other conventional ne'er do wells – it was then.

But so stunning was the hit on America that most New Yorkers, criminals included, sat transfixed in front of their televisions or rushed home in a panic to do just that.

There were exceptions, of course, including Henryk Siwiak. A Polish immigrant with a serious work ethic, Siwiak that night took the subway from his modest apartment in Rockaway Park, Queens, to Bedford-Stuyvesant, Brooklyn, in search of the supermarket where he was to begin his first shift, 8 p.m. to 4 a.m., sweeping and mopping the floor, among other cleaning duties.

Siwiak, in what for him was unchartered territory, made the mistake of getting off at the wrong station, at the opposite end of the neighborhood, and was shot dead as he tried to find his way. His widow to this day thinks her husband's looks, dark-skinned enough to pass for Middle Eastern and clad in camouflage pants, made him the target of a hate crime.

No one has ever been charged.

Across the city, conventional law enforcement as a whole essentially took a holiday. Sure, cops were still responding to 911 calls and still setting up crime scenes for violent felonies. But summons writing and low-level enforcement went by the wayside, at least for a while.

And gun and drug investigations? They were also severely curtailed. Stryker spent the next two months doing 12-hour tours at the Staten Island Fresh Kills Landfill, which had hurriedly been turned into a drop point for about one million tons of World Trade Center material.

The work was painstaking, emotional, even heart-breaking, as those assigned the grim task sorted and sifted through the debris, finding personal items – wallets, photos, firefighters' equipment, cops' guns, plane parts and, yes, body parts.

Stryker by then had four children and to drive each day to the landfill was to know that for all the good in his life the world for his family suddenly felt like a much more dangerous place.

"The worst experience of my life," Stryker called it. "The landfill smelled. The ground was muddy and nasty. Every day seemed cloudy and damp.

"Depressing."

It's impossible to prove, but any cop will tell you the same thing: once the immediate shock wore off, the drug dealers sensed a golden opportunity, took advantage and operated without fear of arrest.

Police work eventually returned to normal, but by then it seemed that Council and Javier thought there were no eyes on them. And why not? For even when, beginning in July 2002, there were a number of drug arrests involving members of their crew, the busts seemed arbitrary, without investigative focus. If there was a long-term investigation, Council and Javier just weren't seeing it. They weren't blinded by their optimism. There was no long-term investigation.

Until the following summer.

That's when a Manhattan assistant district attorney, Anthony Capozzolo, working a wholly unrelated murder investigation – a bar fight involving Mexican nationals – came across some paperwork at the 24th Precinct, the command that covers the Frederick Douglass Houses. The papers detailed the August 2001 murders of Tyrell Williams and Al Cruz.

Intrigued, Capozzolo, the deputy unit chief for the Firearms Traffic Unit, asked questions. Detectives told him what little leads they had went cold after September 11th. The crew members, they said, were as bad as they come, and witnesses were not exactly lining up at the door to provide information.

And, they told him, just a few days earlier, June 14th, 2003, one Cheo Swanson was murdered in the lobby of 845 Columbus Avenue, a building in the same houses. Swanson went by the street name DC, as he was from the nation's capital. He was also known, oddly, as Country. By any name, he was connected to the same drug crew, the detectives told Capozzolo.

As it turned out, Capozzolo knew the prosecutor assigned the case involving Williams and Cruz. And he also knew full well the limitations of catching a murder then having the investigation go nowhere.

In a best-case scenario, a prosecutor gets the case right way, working closely with detectives in those first critical days of the investigation even if there is not yet a clear-cut suspect. Evidence is gathered and shared. Witnesses are interviewed and the prosecutor will provide assistance and guidance, working to secure search warrants and telling detectives what more is needed, not just to make an arrest but to get an indictment and conviction. But when the case goes cold – and this one was February-in-Canada-cold – then, truth be told, the prosecutor turns to other matters until more progress is made.

But Capozzolo had for some time been working on long-term investigations and figured he could kick start the case, especially after learning about the Swanson murder. He took it over from his colleague – she was planning on leaving the job anyway – and began the arduous task of trying to figure out who did the murders and how they and the rest of their drug-dealing cohorts could be successfully prosecuted and imprisoned for a very long time.

Capozzolo knew Stryker from previous investigations. He called Stryker's supervisor and suddenly the probe had new life. They approached the investigation on three levels. The easy part was the historical analysis, going back several years and reviewing all the drug sale arrests from that precinct. Who were the players at the Frederick Douglass Houses? Where were they now? Could they be flipped? What did they know?

"You make a big book and you show the book to any informants you have and you go, 'Tell me who's in the gang,'" Capozzolo said. "Then, you try to build on that by using the informants as cooperators or by using video surveillance – you look for the guys hanging out in front of the buildings or doing hand-to-hand sales."

It became clear fairly quickly, according to Capozzolo, how Council and Javier had risen to power.

On May 5th, 1997, a man named Jamel Walker was shot dead and Christopher Valentin was slashed. Doctors needed more than 100 stitches to close his wounds. Both incidents happened at West 103rd Street and Amsterdam Avenue, on the western edge of the Frederick Douglass Houses.

Shortly before the murder case went to trial, Council and Javier were charged with threatening a witness, Courtney Sweeney. He claimed that Council and Javier had confronted him in March 1998 with a very simple message: testify against Council and you die. Sweeney told Valentin, Valentin went to the authorities and both Council and Javier were indicted for tampering with a witness.

At trial, Council testified, claiming self-defense. He said he was the one threatened with a gun and that it went off during a life and death struggle with Walker.

The jury bit and in January 1999 Council, Javier and Tyrone Council, Tony's uncle, were all acquitted of the murder. Javier was acquitted of the slashing. Four months later, the tampering indictment was dismissed.

Council and Javier walked away full of bravado. And now Council had himself a nickname, TM, or Top Murder, for having avoided the murder conviction.

"After that they took over the project," Capozzolo said. "And those guys who were the competitors basically fled because now these guys beat a murder rap, which, despite what you see in the movies, doesn't really happen very often. So when it does in this case they get a God-like reputation among a bunch of uneducated drug dealers – they beat the government."

As their legend grew so did their influence. The houses? Javier and Council ran the place.

"After they beat the murder, it's like 'The Wire,'" said Capozzolo, referring to the HBO drama about a drug crew in Baltimore. "Al's like 28, 30 years old and he's training the younger guys, 18, 19, 20 years old. The next generation of drug dealers. Al was like Stringer Bell and he had all these younger guys who were like the younger kids on the block in the show."

############

Stryker, meanwhile, had been hit with an emotional haymaker – the death of his father. He had been ill with prostate cancer for some time, so the family knew the end was near. Still, his passing was difficult to handle. But Stryker had the full knowledge that he and his dad had made amends. The father respected the man the son had become. The son saw the wisdom in the father's ways.

Some months earlier, Stryker had a big scare.

His parents had moved to Mobile, Alabama, in 1989. Retirement had treated them well until the good reverend was stricken with prostate cancer. He had hid his illness from his son for a while. Then, after Stryker found out, his father managed to minimize, at least over the phone, how bad he really was.

But during one of his routine phone calls to his parents something was clearly wrong. Mom was out of breath and didn't know why. He promised to call back later to check on her.

That night, as he, his wife and Erica were driving home from Erica's dance recital, Stryker dialed Alabama again.

The conversation was brief.

"I heard someone falling then I heard my father in the background telling her, 'Ruby, get up.' But he sounded weak and he just kept saying that, like he couldn't go over and help her. Meanwhile, I'm yelling for my mother, but she's not answering."

Stryker hung up and called New York City's 911. He identified himself as a NYPD detective and explained his predicament. Minutes later, he was on the phone with a 911 dispatcher in Mobile, then with the sheriff's office.

In between, he kept dialing his parents' house. The immediate response – a loud, steady busy signal – meant the phone was still off the hook. He feared the worst.

He kept calling.

Finally, a voice on the other end. It was the sheriff. Mom had had a heart attack, but the paramedics were there, loading her into an ambulance. Dad, the sheriff said, was a mess.

The next day Stryker hopped a flight to Alabama and made a beeline to his parents' house.

He banged on the front door. Mom, he knew, was at the hospital and recovering. Dad was supposed to be home.

No answer.

More banging but still no answer.

Eventually, the front door unlocked and there was his father. Strong and ramrod straight in his prime, the Reverend Stryker was now a shell of himself, shoulders slouched, unshaven and weak enough to fall over at any moment. He would get even worse, but at that moment he was weaker than his son had ever seen him.

Indeed, Stryker had reached the moment at which all sons and daughters eventually arrive. He realized he would now have to care for those who once cared for him.

"I remember taking him, laying him down on the bed and being so, so mad. I'm yelling and screaming, wondering why he let this get to this point without tell me. Why didn't he tell me?"

Of course, it quickly became clear. The father didn't want to burden the son. And the mother had agreed with the father. Stryker was as mad at his father as his father had been the day he learned his only child was joining the Marines.

So what did Stryker do? He got his father cleaned up, gave him a clean shave and told him in no uncertain terms that it was time for him and his mom to return to New York.

At work, meanwhile, Stryker was on top of his game, despite his personal problems. He and his wife didn't see eye to eye. She was intensely proud of the work he did, and she didn't hide it. The streets were safer because of men like him, and he had a heart, to boot. He was not some cop caricature, reckless and out of control – Rambo with a gun. He was, she long knew, a man who cared deeply about his work and knew that each kilo of cocaine, each gun, really did mean something. One less kid hooked on drugs, perhaps. One less life cut short by a bullet.

Still, while his obsession with the job was great for the NYPD it wasn't necessarily good for him or his family.

There were days when getting out of bed was a major undertaking. And even when he got to work, Stryker's bowel problems were difficult to hide. He'd pull up at work, gather his strength, trick himself into thinking everything was OK, then find a way to get through the day.

Certainly the stress of being an undercover didn't help, what with the long hours and the awful diet – fast food at all hours of the night, if he had time to eat at all.

"He wasn't eating properly," his wife said. "With the hours he worked he wasn't getting home until late at night, or maybe not until the next day. So you're out there eating whatever's available. Fast food. Junk food. It wasn't like he was getting home-cooked food every day because he worked long hours, odd hours."

In the office, Stryker worried that word of his ailment would get around and force him to the sidelines. The fact is cops show up every day with their baggage attached – drinking problems, marital tensions, high blood pressure, heart woes, etc. Often, a boss will look the other way, but Stryker took no chances. Rather than try to completely hide his problem, he told a small circle of colleagues and supervisors about his failing health. They respected him and vowed to do everything in their power to keep his little secret their little secret.

Stryker, in turn, tried to manage his crisis. He made sure not to eat much, if at all, in the hours leading up to a buy. He used the restroom just before heading out on a sting. And, increasingly, he wore adult diapers. It was embarrassing and humiliating. During a shopping trip to Costco, Stryker was convinced the cashier would ask him, loud and in front of everyone, why he was buying a large package of Depend underwear.

"These are not for me," he told the cashier before she had a chance to say anything. "They're for my grandpa."

"It was not easy," Stryker remembered. "There were days where I'd be fine. I'd think, 'OK, I got this. It's getting better.' But then the next day it would be worse than ever. I was still able to concentrate and somehow do whatever I had to do to get through the buy. Sometimes, I'd show up at work and wonder if I'd make it through the day. And there were times I'd have to call in sick, but usually I'd be able to deal with it."

Still, his weakness, his vulnerability, only seemed to contribute to his failings at home. Sure, he was a top-flight undercover, but such work, even in the short term, took its toll. The stories to remember. The shifting identities. The lies to keep straight. The utter danger.

"There is nothing, and I mean nothing, fun and exciting about sitting in a room with a bunch of bad guys, each of them ready to end your life at a moment's notice," Stryker said. "What they never knew was I was in complete control. I could talk my way into and out of any situation. But way too many times I felt bad about it. Conflicted. How can I be this person, this guy with a wife and kids – and I never smoked or drank – and at the same time be a liar, a conniver and a scammer? Not easy.

"And being sick only made things more difficult."

Often, Stryker would drive home, sit in the car and decompress before walking inside to greet his family. Other times, he'd sit in the living room, staring into space. Those were the good days, when Stryker the undercover knew full well he wasn't quite ready to be the family man. Thanks to his upbringing, he didn't party and he didn't drink. He just needed time alone. To review. To reflect. To pray.

But on the bad days, the man walking through the front door was someone else. Charlene, no wallflower, would have none of it and would tell her husband to check his machismo at the door and remember that once he came home he was a husband and a father, not the swaggering drug dealer he played at work.

"After he started doing undercover work, he started to change," she remembered. "He became married to his job. He'd come home and unwind in front of the TV – zone out, you would say. Unfortunately, as he became better and better at this job he would sometimes come home as if he was that undercover, talking like he was dealing with one of the perps and I'd be like, 'Dude, what is wrong with you?' He was like some gangster or hoodlum, and it was frustrating because I didn't know who I was dealing with. He'd have a short fuse and we'd argue and disagree.

"It put a big burden on our marriage."

And yet despite all that Stryker had decided to take on another responsibility, though it was one that would ultimately change the rest of his life for the better.

He wanted to evangelize, to spread the word of God.

Stryker had come full circle, from the child who rolled his eyes when it was time to go to church, to the young man who rebelled and joined the Marines, to the adult who came to more fully appreciate his father and decided to follow in his footsteps.

Charlene wasn't convinced this was the best idea, given the problems they were having. Stryker, naturally, won her over, though his work was still his main focus.

############

So when the call came from Capozzolo, Stryker jumped in the only way he knew how to do things – with both feet. Capozzolo had cultivated a key informant, a drug dealer, who was high up on the crew's food chain but, upon being arrested, was not as loyal as Council and Javier would have hoped. He turned state's evidence, provided Capozzolo a window into the operation and smoothed the way for Stryker to meet Javier.

Sort of like a blind date, only with guns.

"It was one of those cases where I didn't have to work my way up the ladder," Stryker said. "The informant was already at the top."

Good thing, too, as Council and Javier were typically very careful about taking on new customers – and careful in general to avoid arrests. They had lookouts on bicycles. Lookouts on park benches, pretending to relax. Lookouts in front of the building. There were also steerers to get past.

"You had to go through the guys on the bike, the guys on the benches, the guys in front of the building, the guys in the lobby, all to get to the guy in the stairwell who would sell you the drugs," Stryker said. "But the informant cut through all that."

Still, there was much work to be done and little reason to believe this case would be any less dangerous than any other. Indeed, it was important to remain diligent and not to get sloppy.

"Javier was a bad dude," Stryker said. "If he walked in a room you felt it. He had that street swagger. If he walked in with Tony Murder (Stryker liked that better than Top Murder) you would get up and leave. He could kill you at any moment."

The first meeting was set for right outside the projects. Stryker and the informant drove up, parked on the street and waited. And waited. Twenty minutes. Thirty minutes. Forty minutes. Fifty minutes.

Finally, after an hour, Javier arrived. Long beige coat. Hair in two long braids. Distinctive, for sure. The informant got out and he and Javier went up the block to talk. Stryker stayed behind the wheel, preparing for the worst, hoping for the best.

When they were introduced, Stryker laid it out. He was Sisqo – he picked that because he liked the rhythm and blues singer by the same name – he was from Brooklyn and he ran with the Bloods gang. He and his boys didn't like the dealers from further north, in Washington Heights. Dominicans, he said disgustedly, were always trying to rob Stryker or accuse him of trying to scam them. And one other thing: he said in no uncertain terms he was not dealing with his guy, meaning the informant.

"Listen man, this dude, he's always on the move," Stryker told Javier. "He don't answer the phone all the time and I'm always trying to make money. You know what I'm sayin? If I can't get hold of him can I just call you? Cause I hate hanging around."

Of course, that wasn't remotely the case, but Stryker was going right in for the kill – and doing so with the informant right there.

Javier was smart. He was savvy. And he was cunning. But he fell for Stryker's pitch.

"Yeah, yeah, no problem," was Javier's response.

"Right off the bat I was going for the jugular," Stryker recalled. "He knew I was straightforward. Besides, you flash money it makes dudes dumb."

Stryker took out $400 – $50 wasn't gonna cut it when you're dealing with the boss. Javier left, then came back a few minutes later with crack. Done deal.

Of course, Javier could have murdered the informant at that point and Stryker would be kicking himself. Instead, Javier had fallen for the spiel. He took to Stryker, trusted him, sold him drugs that day and continued doing business with him.

At one point, Javier, sitting in Stryker's car, virtually sealed the case against him.

"You see all these guys?" he asked Stryker, pointing to his street crew, his boast captured on an audio recording. "These guys are all mine. You got a problem with them, you come to me and I'll take care of it."

Capozzolo was over the moon.

"Al was basically saying, 'This is a company and I'm the boss.' That's like what you see in the movies. You never see that with cases like that. For that to happen, for him to say that to Stevie, that was huge."

On another occasion, as Stryker was completing a drug buy, a rap song, an ode to drug dealing, blared in the background. The song later provided a moment of levity when audio of the deal was played during the trial and jurors heard the lyrics.

At the time, however, there was no laughing. Each encounter with Javier was fraught with the concern that things could go wrong in a hurry.

Those concerns were justified.

On the day of another planned buy, January 12th, 2005, Stryker maneuvered his SUV into the parking lot. Scottie, another undercover, was sitting next to him. It was winter, early evening. Enough people around that nothing bad would happen. Or maybe it would. Such is the nature of narcotics work, of criminals in general. Javier wouldn't open fire on a crowded street now, would he? With all these witnesses around? But Stryker knew from working this crew for months that neither Council nor Javier worried much about witnesses.

"For some reason, something tells me to take Scottie," Stryker said, referring to a fellow undercover. "Some people called us Yogi and Boo-Boo. He's bigger, so I was Boo-Boo. Good thing I took him, but at first they were pissed. I called an audible without them knowing. I called Javier and he hits me back. It's obvious he's watching me or someone's calling him and filling him in."

"Who's in the car with you?" Javier demanded.

"I got my bodyguard with me now," Stryker said, according to a transcript of the phone call. "I got to carry a big nigga with me, cause niggas is jealous of me now."

Scottie certainly looked the part – 6 feet 2 inches tall, 240 pounds. Like a NFL linebacker.

"That nigga look mad suspect," Javier said.

"C'mon, man," Stryker said. "He's good. He's with me. Look, don't be nervous."

Probably, Stryker figured, Javier and his crew thought Scottie was there to rob them.

"Now I'm starting to get worried because I see these cars going back and forth on the street. They're watching me and Scottie, checking us out, *really* checking him out. Scottie has a gun in his lap and so do I. Then we see this Ford Explorer. It's Council."

Scottie was just as worried.

"Stevie, these guys are circling."

"Oh, yeah."

And Council was not alone.

"He's got three other dudes in the truck. I remember the look he gave. I remember that look. I'm like, 'Oh shit.' I'm on the phone, telling the boss, 'Listen, I just saw Tony Murder roll by in a Ford Explorer and he's got three other dudes in the car.'

"I look at them. They look at me. 'Yo, Scottie, that's Tony Murder. That's their hit man.' Scottie's like, 'They're gonna get hit all right – by us.'"

Javier called again.

"Yo, what's up with your man?" he asked again.

Stryker didn't like the sound of this.

"Yo, I told you, he's with me. What's up with Tony? Why's he circling?"

"Chill," Javier said. "I'm on my way."

At that point, Stryker and Scottie were like sitting ducks. Their heads were swiveling in every direction. Where the fuck was Tony? Javier's coming? From where? Was he with Tony in the Explorer?

"Then, all of a sudden, there are two dudes approaching, on foot, then they split up and we don't see them anymore."

It's wasn't Javier. It wasn't Tony. Lookouts? Undercovers from another operation? Innocents heading home from work?

"At some point your ego kicks in and you're thinking, 'I'm gonna do this. I'm taking these guys out,'" Stryker said. "You got Tony Murder, who never comes out, he's out there and he's circling. Then you got these other two guys walking near us then splitting up. We don't know where they are. Then all of a sudden I see Javier walking. I'm like, 'Yo, he's the first one I'm gonna shoot, yo.'"

Javier looked around, then approached. Scottie stepped out of the car.

"Nah, nah, don't get out," Javier said. "Don't get out."

Scottie knew he and Stryker couldn't let Javier get into the back seat.

"It's cool," Scottie told Javier. "It's you and my man."

Stryker had his gun under his lap. He had never fired his weapon in the field. And he never would. But on that day, he was sure it would come to that.

"All I have to do is lift my leg and pop, pop. And I've already made up my mind that one move and I'm killing Javier. Scottie's in the same position, so this could happen either way, but at the same time I'm watching Scottie and Javier – and this is all in a matter of seconds – I'm watching for the Explorer and I'm watching for the two dudes who came up to us on foot."

But maybe Javier just wanted to check Scottie out. Maybe he was just being extra careful.

"Look," Javier said to Stryker. "I don't know your man. He looks kinda shady."

Stryker had a quick retort.

"And you got your boys circling around. I don't know who those guys are with Tony. And who's the two dudes you got running up on us?"

Javier admitted to this, which was a critical piece of the puzzle. Javier had just put himself at the scene and at what was supposed to be another buy, then linked himself to Tony, to the guys in the car with Tony and to the mystery duo on foot. All important evidence.

Then, without any sign his anger would subside, Javier relented. OK, so Stryker brought a new guy to the table. Javier responded the only way he knew how, with a show of force. All even, he told Stryker. Let's do business.

The deal went down, $2,550 for more than 2 ounces of cocaine. Everyone lived.

Stryker, however, worried what the next buy might bring. He later called Javier to gripe.

"Yo, Al – What's up?" Stryker asked, according to a transcript of the conversation. "We good? All right. Yo, yo, my man was amped about those two cats that you walked off with man. That nigga was like, 'Yo, who those niggas right there?' I told him you was amped about him. Yeah cause he, I know I am good. Yeah, no doubt, cause I'm talking to my man now and he is like, 'Yo, where did the other two niggas come from, yo?'

"He said he concerned about me. He was like, 'Those niggas was up to no good, man.' Said the niggas was up to no good. I said, 'This is my peoples. I have been doing business with them, yo.' You hear what I'm saying, Al?...I ain't coming to rob you…"

By that point, Stryker had helped gather more than enough evidence for an indictment. And other undercovers involved in the investigation had made smaller buys from some of the smaller players. There was more to be done, for sure, more work that would have likely linked more violence to the crew and pulled more players into the mix. Maybe even more information about who was supplying Council and Javier.

But the parking lot encounter raised too many red flags. The last thing the brass at One Police Plaza needed was a dead undercover. The call came down to end the case.

Shortly before a judge signed off on numerous warrants and Capozzolo was given the go-ahead by his bosses to authorize arrests Stryker was again at the Frederick Douglass Houses, riding an elevator with a fellow undercover when on stepped an elderly woman.

She took one look at the cops, made them for drug scum and shook her head in disgust. Stryker chuckled to himself.

"Don't worry, ma'am," he felt like telling her. "Pretty soon you'll have nothing to worry about.

In April 2005, Council and Javier were indicted and arrested on narcotics conspiracy and drug selling charges. Later indictments charged EZ with killing Al Cruz and Tyrell Williams. He was also charged with taking part in a shooting in which his friend, Eric Holmes, was paralyzed by a shot fired by someone else and meant for EZ. Mojica was also charged in Williams' death, accused of acting in concert.

During opening statements, Capozzolo perfectly summed up the crew. He described the stranglehold it had on the houses, cooking crack in several apartments, selling it in lobbies and courtyards and netting over $1,000 a day in street sales to users and thousands of dollars more to other street-level operations and wholesalers in Pennsylvania and Virginia.

"Two men, Al Javier and Tony Council, brought together other mainly younger men in their late teens to early 20s, not to build up a community but to destroy it – all in the name of making easy money by selling as much crack cocaine in their own neighborhood as the customers would buy," Capozzolo told jurors. "Some of the customers were big. Others were small. But the goal was always the same: sell as much as possible and make as much money as possible. All of this was done at the expense of the thousands of other residents of the Frederick Douglass Houses and other nearby residents."

Each and every day, he said, the crew sold hundreds of dime bags, making about $60,000 for each kilo. Even factoring in what the street sellers were earning, Council and Javier were pocketing $40,000 for each kilo sold via dime bags. Then there were the bigger sales, kilos sold to dealers in Pennsylvania, and, as the ringleaders now knew, to Stryker and other undercovers.

"Lucrative is an understatement," Capozzolo said.

Stryker also had his day in court, testifying about his dealings with Javier. At one point, he recounted the mantra for which Javier became known.

"Let me," Javier would tell Stryker, "help you help me."

For emphasis, Stryker turned to the jury. Smart move, as it gave the jurors a sense that they had a stake in the proceedings. The defense lawyer thought differently.

"Excuse me," the lawyer said. "I would prefer you look at me when I'm asking you a question."

"I'm sorry," Stryker shot back, "but my mom and dad told me when you're answering someone to look at the people you're answering to."

Stryker had even turned his chair in the direction of the jury box, and as the lawyer walked past him and pointed this out to the judge a faint whisper could be heard.

"Asshole."

"Your honor, did you hear what this detective said?"

"I didn't call you nothing, sir."

After a six-week trial, the crew's five major players were convicted and sent to state prison. Javier got 40 years to life for conspiracy and drug convictions. Council got 30 to life for drug convictions. EZ got 50 years to life for murder and conspiracy. Mojica, who pleaded guilty to manslaughter and conspiracy, got 12 years in prison. And Michael Wilson, a top dealer, got a seven- to 21-year sentence for conspiracy.

Ten others were convicted and sentenced to shorter prison terms.

Afterwards, outside the courthouse, the defense lawyer walked up to Stryker and extended his hand. An olive branch.

"You're still an asshole," Stryker told him and walked away.

CHAPTER 10 – DANGER

Each day that police officers leave home for work could be their last. For narcotics officers the possibility is much greater. For black narcotics officers working undercover the possibility is greater still. Surprisingly, or maybe not, depending on your perspective on race, the threat faced by minority undercovers buying drugs in minority neighborhoods can sometimes come from their fellow officers.

Friendly fire, they call it when one officer unintentionally shoots another. There is nothing friendly about it.

############

On November 16th, 1776, at the height of the Revolutionary War, Great Britain battled and defeated its 13 colonies at Fort Washington, in Washington Heights, the Manhattan neighborhood north of Harlem. The crushing blow sent General George Washington and his troops in a retreat to Delaware.

Some 200 years later, Washington Heights, by then a teeming, bustling residential neighborhood populated by mostly poor and working class Dominican immigrants, was fighting an entirely different war.

The neighborhood is centrally located – a short subway ride from downtown, a stone's throw from the Bronx and just minutes from the George Washington Bridge, which connects in one direction to affluent Bergen County, New Jersey, and in the other direction to the highways that lead to upscale Westchester County and Connecticut.

Each and every day, at virtually any hour they would come: Wall Street brokers in Lincoln Town Cars; college kids on the A train; suburban dads in their BMWs; desperate housewives in their Mercedes. Add to that the poor and working class who were hooked on drugs and lived in the Heights or travelled there for their fix.

Washington Heights – cocaine capital of America.

In truth, the so-called war on drugs has been at least a bit of a farce, its battles sporadic and uncoordinated, one city doing this, the other doing that. Even the cooperative efforts involving federal agencies working with their state and city partners seemingly did little to make a difference.

Sure, those press conferences you'd see on TV looked impressive, what with all the guns and drugs on the table while a host of politicians and cops stood there as news photographers clicked away. But it often seemed to be little more than window dressing.

Still, you can't just throw up your hands and do nothing. And, in fact, Washington Heights today looks like a different world, increasingly gentrified, as expensive as some parts as the more traditionally unaffordable parts of Manhattan. The reasons are varied. Habits changed, certainly, with prescription drugs increasingly the vice of choice and more dealing done inside and online. And law enforcement got better at what it did. It mixed long-term investigations that dismantled major drug operations with boots-on-the-ground enforcement, busting low-level street dealers whose very presence ruins it for the mom walking her kids to school, the old lady going grocery shopping and the merchants trying to make an honest living.

But in the early 2000s, Washington Heights was blowing up again, not like in the crack years of the late 1980s and early 1990s but enough for residents to complain to police about the street-level drug dealing. At the same time, residents south of the Heights, in several parts of Harlem, were similarly concerned. Eventually, word filtered down to One Police Plaza and the response was unequivocal. It was time for an "All Out." It meant just what it sounded like – an all-out effort to get rid of the problem. All hands on deck. All units working together. Narcotics. Gang. Patrol. Detectives. The Office of the Manhattan District Attorney.

The problem was basic: entrenched dealers in Washington Heights were selling their wares in that neighborhood and were also providing a bulk of the cocaine sold in other parts of Manhattan, especially Harlem.

"No matter what crew you worked for in Harlem, all the drugs were coming from Washington Heights," Stryker said. "So the bosses figured if you shut the pipeline you would dry up those precincts."

But sometimes too many cooks really do spoil the soup. And that's what happened with All Out.

"They flooded the area with uniform cops, anti-crime cops, street crime cops, SNEU (Street Narcotics Enforcement Unit) cops," Stryker said. "Everyone was thrown in the mix. So, it was a good idea but not a well thought-out plan.

"You want to do it right? Remove the uniform cops. That gives the dealers a false sense of security. But when you have all these uniforms out there, yeah it'll cut down on the street dealing but all that does is push these guys inside, which makes it dangerous for who? The undercovers.

Instead of us being able to just walk up to the corner – 'Yo, give me 30 grams' – and walk away, now I gotta go into the building, maybe past a lobby with an extra set of doors. All that gives the dealers that much more time if the cops are coming in. And it's more dangerous for guys like me. Will my kel work? Is there someone hiding in the stairwell?"

Even worse is that without proper coordination, the undercovers can be in an equal amount of danger from other cops. Ideally, the undercovers are introduced beforehand to the various other units taking part in an operation. That's less likely to happen when an initiative is rushed into action.

"That is so important because remember, we don't wear vests. Everyone else has their vests on so people know who they are. Stevie Wonder can see them coming. With us, they don't know who we are. So ideally everyone involved should know what we look like."

Ideally.

############

Stryker's assignment one day during All Out was to chat up an older Dominican dealer, maybe 50 years old.

Stryker had on black sweats – one pant leg pushed all the way up – plus a Cleveland Indians hat, a white baseball jersey and red beads. He was posing as a Blood.

"Yo, Papi, I'm trying to get 30 grams."

Right from the get-go the dealer was suspicious.

"Policia?" he asked. "Policia?"

"Nah, man," Stryker shot back, offended. "I'm not a cop. Come on."

"Look, man," the dealer said. "We gotta go in the building."

Stryker's sergeant heard this on the kel. Not what he was hoping for, though on that day Stryker had a partner with him, Detective Benny Wagner.*

Detective Dave Fryar*, meanwhile, served as Stryker's ghost. He's a big black guy with dreads who stood out like a sore thumb in mostly Dominican Washington Heights. He was nearby, as he should have been, trying to keep Stryker in sight. But he was also raising up suspicion among the street dealers. Was he there to score or was he there to rob them?

"Yo, man?" he was asked. "You buyin?"

Stryker, of course, knew none of this. His job was not to look around for Fryar. He just assumed Fryar was keeping an eye on him.

The dealer led Stryker and Wagner into the building, unlocked the front door with a set of keys and pressed the elevator button. Any back-up response would require getting buzzed in, arriving as someone was leaving, or busting the front door down.

The sergeant needed to know where his men were heading.

"Yo, where we going?" Wagner asked.

The dealer thought nothing of it.

"Sixth floor."

Now the sergeant knew.

Heading up.

Stryker was wearing a belly bag, a corset-like contraption fat people wear to look slimmer. He was reed thin but needed a place to holster his gun.

"But when I got out of the car it must have rose up because now it was to the point where my gun made an outline in my shirt."

The dealer saw this.

"Yo, pistola!" he yelled out. "Pistola!"

"And then the dude reaches for my gun," Stryker said. "Grabs it. He actually has his hand on the handle. Me and Wagner just react and start whooping his ass. We're pounding him out. He's screaming at the top of his lungs."

Down on the street, meanwhile, the sergeant was on the radio, wondering what was happening.

"Where the fuck is Stevie?"

Fryar wasn't quite sure. The inquisition he was getting on the street distracted him. As he explaining that he was simply waiting for someone, Stryker and Wagner had slipped out of view.

He gave the sergeant what he thought was the correct address.

"Situation like that," Stryker said, "Fryar should have just went, 'Yo, I'm waiting for my man to bring me 50 grams. What's the problem? Ain't about you at all. I'm waiting for my man.'"

Back in the elevator, he and Wagner were fighting it out with the dealer, who despite being outmanned was more than holding his own. Screaming for his life, he managed to press any elevator button he could reach with one hand while using the other hand to hold onto Stryker's gun.

"Once he sounded the alarm on the elevator he's yelling in Spanish, 'I'm being robbed! I'm being robbed!'"

The elevator jolted to a halt, giving Stryker and Wagner the chance to gain control of the dealer. Wagner grabbed him by the neck, Stryker by the shoulder.

More importantly, Wagner had his gun out, and Stryker managed to get ahold of his own gun.

"I'm telling Benny, 'When that door opens, we're using this guy as a shield in case he's got someone on the other side, waiting for us.' But when the doors open there's nobody there. Thank God. The suspect broke free and ran off.

Fryar, the sergeant and the field team, meanwhile, were heading to another building. The wrong building.

As the dealer headed down six flights of stairs, Stryker and Wagner gave chase. Looking back, Stryker realized the smart play would have been to run after the guy into the lobby and no further. After that, when the suspect got outside, Stryker should have barked out their address, waited for help, then called it a day.

They got to the lobby.

The dealer made it outside the building.

The adrenaline was flowing.

The undercovers ignored what they knew they should have done and continued giving chase.

"And as I'm running I'm not yelling out the address because I'm thinking my ghost knows what building I ran into."

The dealer reached the corner and turned right, still yelling in Spanish that's he was getting robbed.

"And I have a gun in my hand," Stryker said. "So imagine how that looks."

Wait, there went the field team – heading in a different direction.

What the fuck was going on?

It got worse: a patrol car passed by, the two officers inside unaware of the undercover operation and thus not familiar with Stryker or Wagner.

"The driver makes eye contact with me and he's watching as I'm catching up to the Dominican guy. That guy is out of breath, he's got this hands up and I got my gun literally to his head. As this is happening the two officers in the patrol car are getting out."

Wagner was further back, too far removed to catch the attention of the cops in the patrol car.

Stryker's life, his wife, his children, flashed before his eyes.

"All I hear is, 'Police! Don't move!' I look in their direction and I see an officer in his 3-point stance with his gun drawn. Next thing I hear is, 'Don't shoot! He's a cop! He's a cop!'"

It was Detective Mike Smith, a member of the field team.

Smith jumped between the uniform officer who was about to open fire at Stryker.

Smith was lucky he wasn't killed. So was Stryker.

The next few moments were a blur.

The rest of the field team pounced, seemingly out of nowhere, and took the Dominican dealer down to the ground, cuffing him. Other cops arrived in an unmarked car. They grabbed Stryker – it happened so quick it looked like an abduction – and sped off, maintaining his cover.

The sergeant was there trying to bring the situation under control. Other patrol cops were showing up. Bosses arrived at the scene. It was a first-class shit storm.

Except for the passers-by who couldn't make heads or tails out of what they just witnessed, the whole operation went down without public scrutiny. Not one bullet was fired. The dealer was cuffed and processed without outcry from his family. The media never found out.

But the NYPD reviews every buy to learn from its mistakes and emphasize what was done right. This near miss was analyzed, rehashed and argued about for weeks. Reports. Paperwork. Meetings. Criticisms.

Stryker, to be sure, was not without fault. He knew the moment he exited that lobby and continued to chase the dealer that he was upping the ante, putting himself and Wagner in harm's way. And for what? A 50-year-old guy who challenged them in the elevator. A bit player. And even though any arrest could be the key moment in an investigation the risk wasn't worth it. Stryker knew machismo had trumped reason. And he realized, upon further self-reflection, that he should have told the dealer that if he wanted his money he'd wait down on the street until the drugs arrived. No going inside.

"You never have to make the buy," Stryker explained. "You can walk away. Even when there's pressure to make a bust because it's an important part of the case, as the undercover you have the final say. If it doesn't feel right you can just walk away from the buy, come back another day."

Stryker made sure he told Fryar that he, Stryker the veteran, had made a rookie mistake. But Fryar was determined to kiss undercover work goodbye.

"This is not for me," he told Stryker. "Narco work is not for me."

Stryker wasn't gonna lie. Fryar needed to do a better job handling the street toughs talking shit to him. But he shouldn't quit undercover work. Learn from each case, he told Fryar. This was a near miss but a miss nonetheless. No one was killed. No one was shot.

Fryar stayed. And prospered.

A few years later, after Stryker was off the streets and working as a NYPD instructor schooling new undercovers in training, an officer raised his hand.

"Detective, do you remember me?"

Stryker did not recognize him.

"I'm the guy who almost shot you a few years ago in Harlem."

Stryker walked up to him and they hugged, nearly cried, too, as others in the class, not quite sure what was going on, watched and applauded.

############

The undercover-dealer relationship is very much like a chess match. The one not in control is always in a position of catch-up, with less room for error and less confidence that you can get what you want. You are reacting to the other man's moves rather than have him reacting to your moves.

Heading out to Brooklyn one day, Stryker felt pretty good about things. He was working that day with Detective Jimmy Cavello,* the lead detective in another gun case. Cavello may have been Italian, but his colleagues liked to tease him about "acting black." To him, he was just trying to get the job done by putting on a street smart, tough guy veneer. At 6 feet, 200 pounds and with a likeable personality, he was good at what he did.

"My job that day was more or less not to interact with the seller," Stryker said. "Just lay back, keep an eye on Cavello. So we drive all the way out to Coney Island and we meet this young Hispanic guy. The kid says he doesn't have the guns there. We have to go to Harlem."

Oh.

A curve ball. Not unusual, but such a wrinkle raised a host of questions for the undercovers. Were they being set up? Did Mr. Hispanic know they were cops? Was he trying to figure out where their back-up was? Ideally, the guy would have got in the car, handed over the guns, been given his money and left. A nice, controlled buy, two cops and one bad guy with the windows up and every snippet of dialogue clearly recorded.

But few game plans go exactly as planned. Many go down nothing like they've been laid out in the tactical meeting held before each buy.

Still, an overwhelming majority end with the desired result: a purchase of guns or drugs and not a single bullet fired.

But when things go bad they can have disastrous consequences.

In late August 2015, a Bronx undercover took a call from a gun dealer who had already done business with the NYPD. He had more guns for sale, and so the undercover picked him up. He had $2,200 on him, ready to make a buy and make stronger the already solid case police had developed against the suspect.

But the dealer wanted to go to Mount Vernon, just north of the city line, to do business. Another guy, the dealer told the undercover, had the guns. The undercover could have pulled the plug without raising the seller's suspicion. He decided not to, and he wasn't necessarily wrong to do so.

When the undercover arrived in Mount Vernon, the other guy in question jumped in the back seat, pulled a gun from his backpack and ripped the undercover off, all $2,200.

In the next frantic moments, with the dealer fleeing the scene, the cop pulled his weapon, the gunman refused to drop his weapon and the cop fired, striking and wounding the gunman.

Tragically, a 61-year-old innocent bystander, a God-fearing family man, no less, was also struck. He later died.

So, Cavello and Stryker could have told the seller to fuck off and walked away.

They decided against it and drove to Harlem, but not without reservation. The whole time Stryker was driving, Cavello, sitting in the back behind Mr. Hispanic, complained about having to deal with black guys in Harlem.

"Yo," Stryker shot back. "Have you noticed that I'm black?"

"Ah, man, you're different."

Cavello's rant served two purposes.

One, he was reminding Stryker that their recent buys in Harlem meant another trip up there could blow their cover. It was no small concern, and it's a key reason undercovers only last so long. The job is mentally exhausting, for sure. And after a while there are only so many dealers out there. Eventually, if you don't cover your tracks you will get made as the police or run into someone you bought from, fucked over, locked up, pissed off. Take your pick.

Cavello was also bonding with Mr. Hispanic and figured he'd play the race card to the hilt.

"I don't like dealing with black guys," he tells Mr. Hispanic. "They short you. They try to rob you."

"Nah, nah, we cool. We cool," Mr. Hispanic shot back. "Where we're going, they're my peeps. We're not dealing with no black people. No one's gonna try and rob you."

To be safe, Stryker thought it best his field team, somewhere behind him, knew where this buy would take place.

"Yo, where we going? I gotta know where to get off."

"Seventh and 135th."

"Gotcha. Seventh and 135th."

They got there and, just like Cavello worried, there were 10 black guys out front. Stryker immediately recognized at least one of them, a crack dealer from whom he recently bought.

Stryker pulled his baseball cap down low. The three of them got out of the car and headed to the building.

At that point, the risk was high. If the dealer recognized Stryker it would raise all sorts of red flags with Mr. Hispanic.

You know this homeboy? I thought white boy here doesn't like dealing with the brothers? Why'd you buy from him and now from me? You running a game on me? Or maybe you're NYPD?

Cavello and Stryker exchanged knowing looks. This had disaster written all over it.

But then, just like that, they were in the building, the dealer apparently not recognizing Stryker.

Inside the apartment there was great unease because they heard a lot of noise coming from a back room. Another guy, black, stepped out and looked around.

Cavello nodded. So much for no black guys being involved.

"Wassup?"

"Who brought the white guy?"

Cavello, already sitting, could have chuckled or made a comment.

Instead, he stood up and pulled out his gun.

Stryker, also sitting, froze. He didn't get up.

"I looked out the window just in case I had to jump. That's how bad this felt."

He pulled out his gun, slid it under his thigh.

Mr. Hispanic stepped in and pushed the black guy to the back room, calming him down, telling him everything was fine.

"Stevie," Cavello whispered to Stryker. "If they all come out and come funny, it's on."

Just then, Stryker's phone rang. It was their sergeant, Rob Skellman, who was fully aware from Cavello's kel what was going on.

"What's the number?"

"Five. Gotta go."

The intercom buzzed.

It wasn't Western Union.

Mr. Hispanic came out from the back room and answered.

"Yo, who's those two guys you let up there?" said the voice. "I'm coming up."

There were at least two other guys talking in the background. Were they with this new player or just waiting to use the intercom?

"Now you got God knows how many people in the back room," Stryker said. "Plus, you got a whole crew coming up. Plus, I know one of the guys from outside. Was he coming up?"

Two minutes later there were two loud bangs on the front door.

Nine guys entered casting killer stares at Cavello. One of them was the guy from whom Stryker had recently bought drugs. Remarkably, he still didn't recognize Stryker.

Skellman, meanwhile, was getting ready to send in the cavalry.

"He had a whole bunch of people in there," he said. "Two of them being outgunned by anywhere from eight to 12 people. That's why I called him. I was going to send my team of eight guys in there. Everybody would be put in cuffs, so it would look like Stevie and Cavello were part of the bad guys."

Stryker rolled the dice and tried to play peacemaker.

"He good. He good. He's my white connection."

Cavello agreed.

"It's good. It's good."

The group headed to the back room. Maybe they were discussing who to shoot first. Maybe they realized who Stryker was and decided he must be a cop.

Cavello didn't want to take any chances.

"Stevie," Cavello said. "Let's just go. Let's just open the door and run down the freakin' stairs."

Just then, Mr. Hispanic came back out and cut to the chase.

"You got the money?"

Cavello pulled out $900 and paid the man, who retreated to the back room then re-emerged with a rifle and handgun.

Normally, an undercover would check the gun out to make sure it worked, for legal reasons. In federal court, where authorities have a wider berth, a firearm does not have to be in working order for a suspect to be charged. In New York state courts – and this was a state case – the gun has to be operable.

But at that point Cavello didn't give a shit. Stryker felt much the same way.

They took the guns, ran down the stairs and hopped in their car.

"We were supposed to go back there at some point and buy more guns," Stryker said. "But we didn't want to run the risk that these guys were talking about us, that they knew me or didn't trust Jimmy.

"So we just let it go and never went back – too dangerous."

Skellman breathed a deep sigh of relief.

"They managed to get the hell out of there," he said. "Another few minutes and I was sending everyone in."

CHAPTER 11 – CALLING IT QUITS

By the time Stryker showed up at the Brooklyn office of Doctor Paul Piccione he was at his wit's end.

"What the hell is wrong with me?"

Stryker had battled through his illness since late in his first year with the NYPD. When it was bad, he felt awful. When it receded, he believed it had passed, that it was all good.

Piccione disavowed him of that notion.

Ulcerative colitis was first discovered around 800 B.C. Nearly 3,000 years later, there is still no cure. One can only hope to contain the illness.

It falls into the broad category of inflammatory bowel diseases. It's likely hereditary, and knowing your family history can help. But the illness can skip four, five, even six generations, and in Stryker's case, no one, including his mother, could recall anyone who had the sickness.

Picture a seven-layer cake. Crohn's Disease, the worst of these bowel diseases, affects all seven. Ulcerative colitis affects only one or two layers, but it is still debilitating and wearing.

"It's a defect in your immune system," Piccione said. "The immune system perceives something being wrong with the colon so it just starts to attack it. It's your immune system attacking the colon that causes all the inflammation and all the destruction of tissue. So whether it's something in the air, something viral, the immune system picks it up like it doesn't belong there. When you have a cold or infection your white blood cell count comes up and it starts to try to destroy whatever virus or bacteria is there. But at least there's a resolution.

"In his situation his body does not perceive the fact that this was ever done. It always feels there is something there that needs to be attacked and the body tries to get rid of it and in doing so there are a lot of chemicals that are produced and released that cause destruction of cells and tissues. That's where you get the breakdown of the skin, all the inflammation, the ulcerations, bleeding and so forth."

Having already been to a couple of doctors, Stryker felt he finally had a handle on what was wrong. Fine, he figured. Ulcerative colitis. Give me some pills and I'm out of here.

Not so fast.

Like any other illness, "stress is a trigger," Piccione said, and when he heard the line of work Stryker was in he had the same reaction as the undercover's wife: You might want to consider a less taxing assignment in the NYPD. He told Stryker that his long-term health was very much up in the air. The more damage done to the colon, the greater the likelihood of cancer.

"He came in looking for a quick solution to the problem, but unfortunately once we made the diagnosis that was not the case. These diseases, it's not that you control them. They control you. Stress, nutrition, all play an important part in how the disease acts and the toll it can take on you."

Stryker at first balked at anything that would get in the way of work. An adult, he was entitled to his decision, even as Piccione advised against it. Stryker's wife, supportive as she was, also tried to push him towards recognizing what was clearly the better decision.

But Stryker kept working undercover.

And so, for several years, the doctor worked closely with Stryker, trying "to put the disease to sleep," as the doctor put it, meaning get Stryker into remission so he could manage his illness.

He did so by prescribing different medications – some that block the immune system from attacking the colon, others, like cortisone, that reduce inflammation.

"Once you're in remission you can stay there a year, five years, 10 years, no way of knowing," Piccione said.

Stryker was thrilled. Anything but giving up the job he was born to do. So he tried to manage his illness by taking his medication and watching his diet.

Stress? That was something else. Work had always, even in the best of times, taxed his relationship with his wife. And even the smoothest drug and gun buys were as relaxing as walking through a den of lions with raw meat strapped to his body.

But Stryker figured that he'd deal with that by timing his meals – home-cooked, fast food or otherwise – to his work. Some days he wouldn't eat in advance of planned buys. Other days, when the opportunity to make a buy came unexpectedly, he'd find himself running to the bathroom, holding it in or, yes, relieving himself in the adult diapers he had come to wear more regularly. It was embarrassing at best, humiliating at worst.

Piccione knew from experience that Stryker was fighting an uphill battle. Stryker put his faith in God, touching in the doctor, also a religious man, a chord of understanding. He may be a man of science, but Piccione also believed in the healing power of prayer.

Still, ulcerative colitis won out.

There were days when Stryker would sit in his personal car, parked outside the office, breathing deeply, willing his body to cooperate. Often, it did. Increasingly, though, it wouldn't. He had built up enough working capital as one of department's go-to undercovers and the few supervisors who were aware of his condition had managed to keep it relatively quiet so Stryker could keep working.

Eventually, though, his career as an undercover would end.

In 2006, Stryker was promoted to first-grade detective, the best of the best, the highest honor for an investigator. Many who hold such a title – and there are only about 350 of them in the NYPD – do so by driving a boss around or working a cushy desk job. Stryker earned his stripes on the street.

But at the same time, he was being told by his superiors that it was time to leave the streets, that he had done his work and done it exceptionally well, for longer than most do it. Burnout was a concern, as was the chance that eventually he would get made, recognized, by a dealer he had previously locked up.

There were several such near misses, but each time Stryker was able to talk himself out of harm's way, convincing an inquisitive dealer that he must be hallucinating to think he had seen him before.

Still, it was time. Stevie Gunz was no more. He was off the streets and assigned to train new undercovers.

There were benefits. Gone were the long commutes to upper Manhattan, replaced by a much shorter trip to the same Brooklyn building where he had undergone training. The hours were steadier, daytime hours, almost like he was working a conventional office job. Some days he would bounce from one command to the next, recruiting cops to work undercover, but his new gig was essentially inside, with no more running around.

"I missed the streets," Stryker said. "But just by working every day and by seeing the impact I was having helped me get over that."

Take what you know, he was told early on, and pass it on. In truth, he had been doing just that since he first became an undercover, leading by example, those around him learning just by working with him.

Now, though, the setting was more formal.

"I remember my first day I walk in, all business-like and I go, 'Good morning, gentlemen, I'm Detective Stryker. I'm your instructor.' I remember the looks on their faces, thinking, 'He looks like he's on the job two hours and he's teaching us?'"

Stryker suspected he'd be tested, much like kids torturing a substitute in grade school. But his retort was simple. He was there not because he had a hook at One Police Plaza. He was there because the department felt he could make a contribution. He certainly felt that way.

Stryker's message to would-be undercovers was always simple: If you think you can't do this, you can't. Drop out now and go back to your command. There was absolutely no shame in that, he told them. Undercover work is not for everyone. Sure enough, much the same way would-be undercovers dropped out when he was training to be one, they dropped out when he was teaching.

"I respected those guys who came to me and said, 'You know what? This is not for me.'"

Others, however, excelled in training and became successful undercovers. Stryker couldn't be happier.

"I told them that I couldn't teach them to be cool and I couldn't teach them swag. There has to be something in them that enables you to do this. I told them it's all right to have fear, but you can't be scared. If you're scared, you don't have control. But fear keeps you sharp, keeps you alert. The guys who got it, they made it because they knew how to stay in control. I was just glad I could lead them down that path."

Supervisors were also given basic advice.

"Always listen to your undercover's gut instinct," he told them. "Never pressure them to go inside. Always protect them. Believe it or not I would hear people say, 'Oh, he's just an undercover.' Excuse me, but your undercover is the most important person out there. On the street, when the buy's going down, the undercover is in charge. He's the boss and if you can accept that and listen to the undercover – which is not easy for some bosses because of their big egos – then cases will get made and everyone will look good."

Stryker enjoyed his time in training.

"I was never one to want to work inside," he said, "but I got to see another piece of the puzzle, another way to make a difference."

Stryker also took part in a training video widely used throughout the department. The video was borne out of necessity – and damage control – after the 2006 Sean Bell shooting.

Bell was just hours away from his wedding when he and his friends, Joseph Guzman and Trent Benefield, left a sleazy Queens strip club and piled into Bell's Nissan Altima.

Police, thinking one of the friends had a gun, approached Bell's Nissan Altima. He tried to drive off, struck a detective in the leg, then crashed into a police van before five cops opened fire. Fifty bullets later, Bell was dead and his two friends in the car were wounded.

Detective Gescard Isnora, the undercover who fired the first shots at the vehicle, later testified that Guzman had stormed off from an argument outside the club, vowing to get his "gat," street talk for gun.

But no one in the car had a gun.

And, by many accounts, numerous tactical mistakes by police, starting with a lieutenant who was faulted for not taking control of the situation as it unfolded, set the fatal encounter in motion.

The controversy raged on for several years. Isnora and two colleagues were indicted for manslaughter and reckless endangerment. They beat the rap at trial, but Isnora was later fired, and three colleagues – the two others who were cleared of all criminal charges, plus the lieutenant – resigned. The incident cost the city $7 million, the amount it paid Bell's fiancé, Guzman and Benefield, to settle a federal lawsuit.

Behind the scenes the NYPD moved to better explain to the public the role of undercover police officers and how they operated. A brief, six-minute video – "NYPD Undercovers: Who Are We?" – was created and shown at various community meetings around the city.

On it, two undercovers, Stryker and Leroy Dressler, are seen, their faces shrouded in darkness, talking matter-of-factly about what they do, why they do it and the dangers they face.

"Who are we?" Stryker asked on the video. "I consider us the antidote for the drug problem in our communities. What am I? I'm an undercover. Where the drug dealers are standing on the corner, where the drug dealers are standing in the lobby, where the drug dealers are dealing in the park – my job is to go into those areas and into those communities and to remove those dealers from the corners, out of the lobbies and out of the communities.

"That's what we do and that's who I am."

He also referenced the tense showdown with Al Javier during the Frederick Douglass Houses investigation. And to connect him further with the ordinary New Yorkers who would watch the video he talked about his upbringing, holding his parents' hands as they walked as one past the dealers who were a fact of life on his block and throughout Bushwick.

"That's why an undercover is out there – to move the drug dealer, not the family. The family has a right to be there. The drug dealer doesn't."

The video was a reassurance to Stryker that he could still be effective working inside. His transfer to training wasn't just window dressing, a soft landing for someone too sick to work on the streets, but rather just the next step in his career.

Still, it was short-lived, a little more than a year. His health was better than when he was buying guns and drugs, but it was still deteriorating to the point where Piccione again had to stress the worst-case scenario.

"I told him that he has to make a choice," Piccione said. "What's going to be really important to him in life? Is it going to be his job or is it going to be his family? He was not really getting better and ultimately it was going to get worse or interfere with his family life."

By January 2008, Stevie Gunz was a goner, resigned from the job he loved. There were too many sick days, too many days where he worried whether he'd complete his tour and just too many days were he was sick and tired of being sick and tired.

Stryker could have collected a disability pension, one that would be tax-free and significantly more than a conventional pension. Certainly, he could have argued the stress of the job caused or at least exacerbated his condition. And certainly his time at Fresh Kills Landfill, sorting through the body parts and debris after the September 11th terror attack, didn't help his illness.

But Stryker had always scoffed at those who tried, in his estimation, to game the system to their advantage. He had no interest in any of that.

"I was done," he remembered thinking. "I love the job, love doing what I did, but I just couldn't do it anymore. I chose my family."

CHAPTER 12 – GOD

Stryker's retirement party was unusual for the number of brass in attendance. Typically, the big bosses showed up for each other – commissioners, deputy commissioners, chiefs and inspectors. First-grade detective was nothing to snicker at, but still, Stryker wasn't a member of the NYPD hierarchy. Nonetheless, they came out. They drank. They ate cake. They tipped their hats. And they thanked him for a job well done.

The next day they got up and went to work. Stryker got up, had breakfast with his wife and began the first day of the rest of his life. He had a new boss now: Jesus Christ.

############

Religion had always been a force in Stryker's life. Even when he hated it – those days and nights helping out in his father's church while his friends were running the streets – it was there. And it certainly served him well as an undercover. He didn't wear it on his sleeve, but when he stopped and prayed before or after making a gun or drug buy, it was all part of his process. He had God on his side, he felt, and what could be better than that?

When Stryker first told his wife he wanted to evangelize she saw it as yet another thing to which he would pay more attention.

"We were having a lot of difficulties so when he brought this up I looked at him with a sideways face," she remembered. "I felt like we needed to work on our marriage first. However, being the wife that is supportive – I supported his career, even when I didn't like him working undercover – I stood behind him."

Besides, some two years earlier, Charlene, who was raised Catholic but was never overly religious, had started attending church with him more regularly. Maybe, she thought, this would benefit their marriage. At least they would spend more time together.

In 2002, Stryker had been formally ordained as an evangelist. He was affiliated with the Bay Ridge Christian Center, a Pentecostal church in Brooklyn, but he also had connections to different churches, including one in Jersey City. He would speak whenever he could, whether at Mass, a hospital, a woman's shelter or a community event.

His wife was also ordained as an evangelist. As a cop, Stryker tried – not always successfully – not to discuss his work or bring the job home with him. As an evangelist, he and his wife drew closer. They often appeared together to spread the word of God. Ultimately, their bond was strengthened.

Still, as long as he was an undercover, that was all a side job for Stryker. But it felt like a natural fit when he left the NYPD.

"With the Police Department there really is no separation of church and state," Stryker said, mocking those who believed otherwise. "It's in the Bible. The Bible said to obey the laws of the land. The Bible also said that God put these people in the position of authority so when you're breaking the law, when you're going against authority, you're actually going against God."

By 2006, with the Strykers' marriage on more solid ground, they decided to branch out on their own and together they founded their ministry, the Empowerment Evangelistic Ministries, Inc. Charlene, a former assistant principal, admittedly had her reservations, but in time they were no longer there.

Then again, the ministry wasn't there, either. At least in the literal sense, it couldn't be found. There was no physical location, just a post office box to accept mail. The church was wherever the Strykers were preaching that day. Some days it was at a Best Western hotel. Other times it was at their home.

"I actually caught myself testing God," Stryker said. "I thought to myself, 'Lord, if you're really with me I'm gonna transform my living room into a house of worship every Sunday.' We went from about six people to 30 people in a few months. And we kept growing, so I told my wife whatever money we collect we'll use for a down payment for an actual church."

In the meantime, they changed the name of the ministry to New Wine Fresh Fire Temple.

In Luke 5:36-39, Jesus said, "No one puts a piece from a new garment on an old one; otherwise the new makes a tear, and also the piece that was taken out of the new does not match the old. And no one puts new wine into old wineskins, or else the new wine will burst the wineskins, and both are preserved. And no one, having drunk old wine, immediately desires new, for he says, 'The old is better.'"

Stryker most definitely qualified as new wine, not your typical man of God, yet he admired his father and his old school ways. And he realized that when he was on the altar he was very much like his father. He was determined to respect the word of God and bring into the fold the old as well as the young.

############

Still, police work wasn't completely in his rear view mirror. He kept in touch with his brothers and sisters in blue, spoke regularly with the prosecutors he considered his friends and followed the NYPD in the newspapers. He even received from the Federal Drug Agents Foundation its "True American Hero Award" in recognition of his "dedication and valiant heroic efforts."

But with a more regular schedule and more dinners at home – his wife, of Puerto Rican descent, wowed him with her rice and beans – Stryker was feeling better than he had in a long time.

He had even accepted an offer, eight months after his retirement, to spend 10 days in Africa – villages in both Kenya and Rwanda – spreading the word. And so he went, the stranger in a strange land using his words not to put people behind bars but rather to inspire people to put their trust in God – to be the person who would never wind up behind bars.

Back home, Stryker figured if he could wow them on the other side of the world, he could wow them in New York City, even more so if he became a pastor. Being a pastor, Stryker knew, meant being able to follow his own vision, not someone else's.

As a minister, you're beholden to the pastor. Maybe the pastor wants you to be the youth minister. Maybe the pastor wants to put you in charge of the worship music. Maybe they pastor thinks you're not ready for a Sunday sermon. Thinks you have to bide your time.

As Stryker put it, "The pastor is like the police commissioner. A minister is like a chief or the head of narcotics. They're important jobs, but they still have to answer to the commissioner. The commissioner is still the boss. He's the one who lays out the mission for the department."

Stryker's mission would be simple: preach the word of God to all those who were willing to listen. It wouldn't be easy, not when people, especially young people, were making church less of a priority. But Stryker was determined, even as he vowed not to come across as overbearing. Stryker saw that as a cop. He worked with a detective who wore his religion on his sleeve and forced his opinions and beliefs on those who had no interest in listening. Eventually, people tuned him out.

But of course becoming a pastor meant much more responsibility: raising money, building a church, or at least moving into a building that could serve as one, paying bills, keeping the place clean. This God business, Stryker knew, was no easy job.

"It's easier to be an undercover detective," Stryker joked.

Stryker's pension allowed him a decent lifestyle, but at that point he and his wife had five children and were in no position to build a church.

Instead, he gave New Wine its first permanent home, in a storefront on Staten Island's Broad Street. It was right across from the Stapleton Houses, home to Ronell Wilson, the gangbanger who murdered detectives Nemorin and Andrews.

"Why did I get a place there?" Stryker asks. "Because I knew I would have a greater impact there. I had Bloods and Crips coming to church on Sunday. I even had a Crip who stabbed somebody in the Stapleton Houses call me while he was on the run. I called an old contact of mine with the Police Department and arranged for this young man to turn himself in. The kid trusted me and so did other kids I talked to. I would stand in front of the church and they would walk by.

"I would say, 'You don't have to join the church but you can always use a prayer' and some of them would say, 'You know what? You're right.' And they'd come on in."

Stryker didn't hide his police background. In fact, he went out of his way to promote it, hoping to inspire someone, even one kid, to live life the right way.

"It was a surprise to a lot of people – 'You were a cop and now you're a pastor?' But I tried not to be holier than thou. I simply let them know that no matter what they did they could always go to God for forgiveness."

Beyond that, the storefront church became a community center. House of worship, yes, but it was also a place to go for backpack giveaways and food drives as well as neighborhood forums on issues of concern to the neighborhood.

The storefront after more than a year proved too small a location, so Stryker expanded the church to the building next door. Eventually, as more and more congregants made Stryker their choice for pastor, and as the weekly donations grew, Stryker was forced to relocate to a larger building a few miles away.

There, his congregation continued to grow, little by little, 50, 75, 100, 200. He had succeeded, for sure, but like a cop, a pastor's work is never done. Problem solved? Here comes another one. You've given guidance to a young man who needed help? Guess what? Now his cousin needs help. That older woman who came back to the church after all these years? Well, she just lost her job and doubts that God is really looking out for her.

At home, Stryker was still dealing with his health issues. Retiring from the NYPD had done wonders for his body, but he was quickly learning that flare-ups would continue to be the norm, not the exception. And he worried each day about his wife, who struggled with fibromyalgia, a chronic disorder that causes body pain and fatigue. She also had developed rheumatoid arthritis and had stopped working to raise their children full-time.

Worse, his mother, who lived in a nursing home and suffered from dementia, was in increasingly failing health.

In late 2014, she died. Her funeral service – a boisterous, hand-clapping celebration of her life, took place at the Bay Ridge Christian Center. Leroy Dressler, himself now a man of God, was the minister of ceremonies. Stryker also spoke, poignantly, about the woman who helped shape him.

Soon after, he and his family moved to a different state, where he soon hopes to establish another house of worship.

"This is who I am now," he said. "My health is good. I still have my moments. There's still concern there, but I couldn't keep working undercover. Now the Lord is my work.

"When I'm up there in front of a group of people it feels like home, like it's where I should be."

THE END

ACKNOWLEDGMENTS

We would like to thank our wives, children and other family members and friends for their support in writing this book. Their encouragement cannot be measured.

Special thanks also goes to former Manhattan assistant district attorneys Anthony Capozzolo and Jordan Arnold, both of whom provided insight, guidance and critical information about some of the cases to which Stryker was assigned. Arnold's brother, Dave, was instrumental in bringing artist Ryan Scully aboard. His amazing work graces the front of this book.

Stryker would also like to thank another assistant district attorney, Dan Rather. The son of the CBS newsman, Rather the prosecutor worked closely with Stryker on a number of gun cases. He is also thankful for the help provided by prosecutors Bruce Wenger, who died in April 2016, and John Arlia on numerous narcotics cases.

Stryker owes a great deal of gratitude to Doctor Paul Piccione, who brought him back to good health, and to the various members of the clergy and houses of worship that have shaped his spirituality, most notably the Bay Ridge Christian Center.

Kati Cornell, who each days handles media inquiries as a spokeswoman for New York City's Office of the Special Narcotics Prosecutor, went above and beyond, answering questions and providing information about the Predicate case.

Some of Stryker's colleagues mentioned in the book also served as consultants, helping to recreate critical incidents in various cases. They include now-retired Detective Mike Paul as well as others who are identified by pseudonyms, including Sergeant Robert Skellman, Detective Leroy Dressler and Detective Jimmy Cavello. Still others helped shape Stryker's career, particularly those he came of age with as a young Transit police officer and those he worked for and side by side with, including members of the Firearms Investigations Unit and different units and bosses, including Inspector Kenneth Cully.

Stryker also wanted to cite a number of police commanders who influenced him, encouraged him and ultimately made him a better police officer.

Most notably, he'd like to thank current Police Commissioner Bill Bratton, who unknowingly inspired Stryker to join the Transit Police Department after transforming it in the early 1990s, and the man Bratton succeeded, Raymond Kelly, whom Stryker hopes and prays one day runs for public office.

Others include current Chief of Department James O'Neill, former Chief of Department Joseph Esposito, and former Chief of the Organized Crime Control Bureau Anthony Izzo.

Parascandola would like to thank Michael Palladino, the president of the NYPD's Detectives' Endowment Association, for recommending Stryker be interviewed for a *New York Daily News* series on gun violence that resulted in this book. Colleague Larry McShane helped greatly with the profile of Stryker and Managing Editor Robert Moore oversaw that and other stories in the series.

Fellow police reporters John Doyle, Anthony DeStefano and Leonard Levitt provided encouragement and recommendations. And former Newsday colleague Sean Gardiner, now an investigator, improved the final product by pointing out all the unnecessary commas and clichés and by making important suggestions. Just as important was Officer Sebastian Danese, the author of a fine book about Superstorm Sandy, "The Battle for Breezy Point." His advice was critical and greatly appreciated.

ABOUT THE AUTHORS

Stevie Stryker was born and raised in Brooklyn. In 1992, he joined the Transit Police Department, which later, with the Housing Police Department, merged with the NYPD. As an undercover officer, Stryker made dozens of gun buys and hundreds of narcotics buys and was acknowledged numerous times for his work in dismantling notorious drug crews and busting prolific gun dealers.

Illness forced him into early retirement in 2008.

Today, he and his family live out of state. The son of a Pentecostal minister from Alabama, Stryker now walks in his father's footsteps, preaching the word of God as a minister.

Rocco Parascandola was also born and raised in Brooklyn, where he lives with his family. He studied journalism at the Brooklyn campus of Long Island University and has worked for New York City newspapers since 1989 – the *New York Post, New York Newsday* and the *New York Daily News*, for which he is currently the Police Bureau Chief, covering the NYPD from inside police headquarters.

He has won the Nellie Bly Award, given by the New York Press Club for best young reporter, as well as team coverage awards for a Manhattan plane crash, the chokehold death of Eric Garner and the execution of two police officers in Brooklyn.

34613982R00103

Made in the USA
Middletown, DE
29 August 2016